Thinking about

SEX AND LOVE

Thinking about

SEX AND LOVE

A Philosophical Inquiry

J.F.M. HUNTER

St. Martin's Press/New York

Originally published in Canada by Macmillan of
Canada, a Division of Gage Publishing Limited.

Library of Congress Cataloging in Publication Data

Hunter, J. F. M.
   Thinking about sex and love.

Includes appendix

1. Sexual ethics.   2. Intimacy (Psychology).
I. Title.
HQ31.H974   1980   176   79-27352

ISBN 0-312-800-18-5

Printed in Canada

First publication in the United States 1980

Cover by Frank Newfeld

Design by Susan Weiss

Contents

PREFACE

This book got its start in life when, after a conversation with a neighbor about the peculiarly factual nature of the courses in sex education that are given in Ontario schools, I was challenged by him to write something that might help people, not necessarily just students, to think intelligently about the questions of values that are involved in the way we conduct our sex lives.

My reaction was that it might be an interesting project, but it was not really my line of business. I was not sure it was philosophy; it was not an undertaking for which my training fitted me; and it seemed to me I would do best to stick to the things I knew something about and was good at. My friend was quite cross about my refusal. "That is what puts me off about you academics," he taunted me. "You have a lot of intelligence and ability, but when you are asked to put it to work on something that matters to people, you shy away and retire to the safety of remote problems and subtle distinctions."

I was quite shaken by his vehemence. While I am just as fond of "remote problems" as most other philosophers, I have always tried to write in such a way as to make my deliberations about them accessible to people without a philosophical training, and have thought of myself as pursuing the remote questions only because consideration of closer-to-hand problems required it.

Yet not only had I never in fact demonstrated that any of my philosophical conclusions had practical applications, but I was, like most philosophers, embarrassed and at a loss if asked how I, as a philosopher, would answer a basic moral question. If someone said, "Come now, you claim to know something about ethics. Show me whether it would be wrong of me to make love to my friend's wife," I would have an opinion all right, especially if he provided me with more of the supposed facts of the case, but nothing I would care to represent as a *philosophical* answer to his question. I would perhaps tell him that we could certainly discuss his question, and my philosophical training might help us to keep the discussion orderly, but it would be primarily as a human being, not as a philosopher, that I would participate.

Many philosophers share this deep aversion to representing moral advice as philosophy, and probably their persistent refusal to help people resolve their moral quandaries is one of the reasons why philosophers are often held in low esteem. Yet I, at least, have never had the reason for this aversion explained to me. Rather, I think, it rubbed off on me, from such things as the repeated experience of seeing how pained a philosopher is when taxed with a direct moral question, or when an answer to such a question is represented as being philosophy.

It is possible, however, to suggest some fairly imposing reasons for this philosophical reticence. In the first place, unless one can prove moral propositions, it may be difficult to avoid the implication that a philosopher's views must be accepted just on his authority. It seems to be implied that since he has thought a lot about these things, while he may sometimes be wrong, anything he says deserves more initial respect than the opinion of someone who is not a philosopher. Such an invidious position is certainly to be avoided.

A second reason might be that moral problems are so individual that it may be doubted whether one can say anything about them that is sufficiently general to be offered as a philosophical contention. What it is best to do will vary indefinitely depending on such things as which persons will be affected, whether any of them have a particular right not to be adversely affected, how likely various possible effects are and what alternatives to a proposed course of action are possible. Hence it is best to consider them singly so that their individuality can be most fully respected, offering any suggested conclusions in a suitably tentative way, recognizing that they might need to be withdrawn or modified upon the discovery of further relevant considerations. This can readily be done in person-to-person discussions of real cases, but in a book, if it is to have any general application, cases lose their individuality, arguments lose their elasticity, and conclusions harden into doctrine through being set down in cold print.

Upon reflecting in this way, my reluctance to take up my friend's challenge was if anything intensified, but moved partly by his indignation and partly by my own longstanding wish that philosophy might yield some practical benefits, eventually I came to think that perhaps there were ways around these difficulties.

The individuality of cases can be respected by stressing that a given conclusion holds at most only for the case as specified, and by indicating ways in which the conclusion could differ if the case differed. The tendency for what one says to harden into doctrine can be avoided (or minimized) both in those ways, and by carefully representing all contentions as having only so much warrant as has been specified, and as being alterable by counter-arguments or further considerations. The tendency to endow a claim or a conclusion with the authority of philosophy can be eliminated by explicitness of argument: the authority for any contention is not that it is the opinion of a philosopher, but is confined to, and as good as, the arguments adduced.

That is the character I have tried to give to the moral deliberations that constitute a large part of this book. While I have taken some stand on all the moral questions I have discussed, I have always defended it with arguments, and have not represented any conclusion as having a greater authority than is to be found in these arguments.

Since there is so much disagreement about sexual morality, I am sure that I will be found too radical by some and too staid by others, and that some sophisticates may be amazed at the naive way I proceed, never doubting that there is some answer to these questions. If my views prove unacceptable to people I will be sorry, because it seems to me that taken together they constitute a civilized approach to these matters, which preserves what we care about most in human relations: responsibility, candor, respect for persons and concern for human welfare. Yet I am less anxious to convince anyone of particular points, than to display as instructively as I can the workings of a way of deliberating about moral questions that can be learned by anyone willing to invest the effort.

While it might be thought that if my method yields unacceptable conclusions it must be faulty, I suggest that on the contrary the method may be accepted while many of the conclusions I have reached are rejected. There is a different relation here between method and conclusion than there is, say, between a recipe and the cake we make using it. If we don't like the cake it makes, then next time we don't use the recipe. The recipe is not meant as a way of deciding whether the cake is good; that question is properly decided in quite other ways. But methods of deciding are meant as ways of getting things right, and there is no way independent of them of ascertaining whether we have indeed got things right. Whereas, if we do not like a cake and are experienced cooks, it does not make sense to bake another according to the same recipe and see if we like it better, if we have doubts about a moral conclusion it makes perfectly good sense to reconsider it using the same methods, because there may be facts we overlooked, or the significance of which we did not appreciate, and we may have been so intent on the benefits accruing from a course of action that we forgot about a way in which our plan might involve deception or be unfair to someone.

Hence I wish to suggest the most appropriate attitude with which to read what follows will be one in which the reader is less interested in whether he agrees with the conclusion than in whether he can find something wrong with the argument. A reader whose first thought is to get to work on the argument will have acquired the disposition that it is my primary ambition to encourage.

J. F. M. Hunter
Toronto, June 1980

INTRODUCTION

In the last two decades, we have passed through a period of rapid and drastic change in our attitudes toward sex. Not very long ago, the widely accepted view in cultures dominated by Western European traditions was quite simply that sexual activity should be confined within the bounds of marriage. There have always been dissenters from that view, as well as people who believed it but did not always act accordingly; but it was the dominant line of thinking about sexual morality, and was solidly entrenched in our culture. It showed in the laws on divorce, in the property rights of women and in the legal status of persons born outside of marriage. It showed in the ways girls were brought up, the vocations that were closed to women and the levels of pay and promotion of women in vocations that were not closed; and it showed in the censorship of books, films and plays and in what was regarded as daring and naughty even by people who rejected the official morality.

The monogamous principle, as we might call it, was so entrenched in our culture that it was not just a moral opinion that many people held, but something very difficult, both psychologically and practically, to reject. So many aspects of life conspired to support it that people who dissented would still find themselves intrigued by the sinfulness of forbidden behavior and a little guilty about their own behavior; and even if they did not, they would encounter manifold obstacles and disadvantages to leading the kind of sex life they preferred. They would have difficulty finding lovers who both shared their views and were congenial in other ways; they would find themselves gossiped about and rejected by people they might otherwise have liked to have as friends; if a dissenter was a woman, she would come to be regarded as "loose" and be the object of unwanted interest on that account; and dissenters generally would suffer from belonging to a category for which there was no accepted place in the system.

That is changing now, but it has not completely changed; and not surprisingly the transitional period has generated its own strains and tensions, some of which have been very painful.

There are people who scarcely question the old way of thinking, never doubt that those who reject it are immoral, and react sometimes with sorrow, sometimes with rage, at what they regard as the decay of our moral values. These people are, one might say, unable to make the distinction between doing what one knows to be wrong, and changing one's opinion as to what is wrong. It seems so obvious to them what is right, they cannot believe that it is not just as obvious to the person who holds a different view, and they can only conclude that such a person is insincere. For them the only tests of what is right are the beliefs they hold, and consequently any departure from those beliefs will be a change for the worse.

There are many people, secondly, who, while they do not entirely accept the old values, have nothing to put in their place, and so have no clear and confident view of how best to conduct their lives. When confronted with a confident traditionalist, they perhaps cringe a little, uncertain whether he may not be right; and even if they do stand their ground, they may have little to say in their own defence. Hence they appear to the traditionalist merely wayward and misguided, and so reinforce him in his inability to distinguish between doing what one knows to be wrong and changing one's opinion as to what is wrong.

Thirdly, there are people who must have some guiding convictions, and finding little in the vacuum left by the passing of the old values that will satisfy this requirement, fasten on some engaging ideal, not always well worked out, such as that of a life of gentleness, affection, music and flowers. The early hippies would be an example, but so too would be anyone who, whether privately or in concert with some like-minded people, adopts as a way of life a similarly simple and good-hearted ideal. The consequences can be difficult. These people will often find themselves quite out of tune with the rest of the community, and the moral earnestness with which they have adopted their lifestyle will tend to make them immune to rational persuasion. Whereas the moral sceptic may often at least be moved by prudential considerations, this type of idealist may think of themselves as devotees of a higher morality, and hence see it as improper to allow prudence to affect their thinking about how to live.

Again, some people will react to the breakdown of old values with radical scepticism: taking the view that not only is it a mistake to affirm the old principles, it is a mistake to affirm *any* principles, whether about sex or any other human concern. Sceptics of this kind will smile patronizingly when a moral discussion of any kind or on any subject arises. This in turn will render other people quite impotent to persuade them of anything whatever, and that impotence, turning as it will to rage, will further estrange elements in the community, and encourage irrational and sometimes violent reactions.

Much of this turmoil is the effect of a rather special problem that besets our practical thinking in times of moral change. In more tranquil times, when there is a moral disagreement, it is usually perceived as a question of whether a mistake has been made in the use of the commonly accepted method of deciding these matters: of whether there is misinformation about the facts or faulty distinctions have been drawn, or operative principles have been overlooked. In such times it may quite often happen that a disagreement is handled confidently and resolved without rancor, because people are in fundamental agreement about the procedure for deciding, and regard themselvs as just needing to be careful how they apply the procedure in the great variety of different cases that can arise.

Times of moral change, however, seem to bring the decision procedure itself into question. People who come to moral conclusions that are very different from any the procedure normally yields will hardly seem merely to be rectifying mistakes in the use of the common way of deciding, but rather to be instituting a new decision procedure, with an implied claim that it is to be preferred to the old method. We seem therefore to be presented with a new kind of question: not "What is the best thing to do here?" but "What is the best way of deciding what is the best thing to do?"

The common ethical wisdom, however, does not include any way of deciding which is the proper or the best way of deciding, and hence we do not know how to handle this new kind of disagreement. Not only have we not, as part of our moral upbringing, been taught any way of handling it, there *is* no recognized way that we might have been taught. There conceivably might have been a way of deciding between ways of deciding which was not generally disseminated because it was too difficult for most people, and not likely to be needed by the average person; but in fact if anyone has such a system, its suitability is not generally recognized, and it is itself as much in need of a way of deciding as to its suitability, as are the competing techniques between which it is supposed to adjudicate.

It will be a serious shock to anyone who has been living in morally placid times to be confronted with the kind of disagreement that seems to raise fundamental doubts about his whole way of thinking about moral problems. Having no way of coping with these doubts, he may lose all confidence that there are rational ways of thinking about moral questions, and this in turn may encourage him to resort to nonrational methods.

Such are some of the dimensions of our present state of moral bewilderment: a widespread loss of confidence in the old values unaccompanied by any clear perception of what might replace them; a variety of responses to the resulting social confusion; a tendency for the responding parties to isolate themselves, and hence for resentments and differences to become intensified; an inability to bridge the differences with candor, flexibility and intelligence, and a consequent tendency to rage, sulk and declaim. Many of us have lost any confidence we ever had that moral questions can be frankly, fairly and profitably discussed; and this is one of the gravest illnesses of our time. Not many people care to embark on the discussion of a moral question, fewer still know how to conduct such a discussion with skill and aplomb, and those who do attempt it are very often met with patronizing smiles or with impatience, as if to say, "Haven't you learned that ethics is an emotional and not a rational affair; that we all have feelings about these things, but to *argue* about them is on a par with arguing that oysters are delicious? If someone doesn't like oysters, he may later come to like them, but never as a result of arguments."

This attitude of course has a self-confirming tendency, because if few people believe in the possibility of rational discussion, it will not often be attempted, and few people will learn to do it well. Not only will they not improve their skills with practice, they will suffer from a shortage of examples from which they might learn. When this scepticism prevails, people on the one hand pursue unpleasant and counter-productive methods of resolving moral disagreements, such as oratory, insinuation, anger and psychological conditioning, and on the other hand tend to be willful and inflexible about their own moral attitudes, treating any criticism as merely the expression of an emotion at odds with theirs, no more deserving to be taken seriously than conflicting tastes in food or fun.

It may be that only the passage of time will get us through this painful period. That is how a great many human problems are disposed of: things look very black for a time and no one knows what to do about it; but a few years later we realize that, without anything having been done to solve the problem, it has resolved itself, and can be forgotten. However, it might either accelerate the cure or at least relieve the symptoms if there were some way of thinking about and discussing our differences that could be conducted calmly and rationally, and that would be capable of altering a person's moral outlook regardless of where he stood on the ethical spectrum. This is what will be attempted here.

Before making a proposal as to how this might be done, it may be useful to say something more about what is required. In the first place, not just any method that will affect attitudes will do. Artful ridicule of people's behavior may often discourage them from acting that way, but will have no tendency to show that so acting would be wrong. We are looking for considerations that serve the latter purpose. Secondly, although various methods of argument, if accepted, may provide ways of demonstrating that an action is a good thing or a duty, and so on, not every such method is morally sound. To take an unreal example: if we had the principle that on the second Tuesday of months with the letter R in them, masturbation is sinful if the moon is full, and not otherwise, we would have a workable method of settling moral questions about masturbation, but clearly not a sound method. We want a method that is not only workable but arguably sound. Hence we will need not only to describe a method of reaching moral decisions, but to relieve doubts as to its suitability.

Here a further complication must be introduced: the method that is going to be illustrated is in fact by no means so short or so clearcut as the imaginary way of thinking about masturbation. Nor is it so finely designed as to enable us to answer every conceivable moral question. Hence it is best explained through extended examples of its employment; and even given such examples, many doubts about it may remain and need to be discussed.

Two distinct kinds of operation will be carried out then:

1. In Chapters 1 to 4 a representative sample of issues in the area of sexual morality will be discussed, and the aim will be to demonstrate, through extended examples, that fruitful and rational deliberation about these questions is possible.

2. Chapter 5 will be an attempt to counter various doubts, not

about the detail of the way moral questions were handled in the earlier chapters, but about the overall method itself. Here we will be dealing with the debilitating and fundamental perplexities about the moral scene that, it was suggested, arise most naturally and most urgently in times of moral change. Since people who are in the grip of these perplexities cannot consistently participate in moral thinking, or perform or avoid actions as being virtuous or otherwise, it can make a considerable difference whether these doubts are allayed. It may be useful to indicate the kind of approach to them that will be taken.

These perplexities arise (it will be maintained) from misunderstandings of a general kind about the moral scene, and are to be removed by showing, not how the problem can be solved, but that it was a mistake to pose it, and that it does not require a solution. These problems are not solved, but dissolved.

For example, a very familiar kind of general perplexity arises from being troubled by the amount of divergence and conflict there is in people's moral attitudes, and by the stubbornness with which people persist in their convictions. One may then ask, "Who is to decide what is right?" Then, unable to accept Plato's answer ("Anyone who has beheld the Forms"), or Hobbes' ("The Sovereign"), or the Church's ("God"), one may conclude that no moral claims deserve to be taken seriously.

We might try to *solve* this problem by shoring up Plato's answer to the question who is to decide, or Hobbes', or the Church's, or by casting around for another arbiter; but we might better try to *dissolve* it by raising the prior question whether it is not a mistake to think that the solution to the problem of moral disagreement can lie only in finding an arbiter with suitable credentials.

We could go on to suggest that the problem has been misperceived: it arises from taking people's moral convictions, rather than the reasons they may have for them, to be basic or ultimate. If the convictions are assumed to be ultimate, there will be no way of mediating between them by any form of deliberation, and hence no other way of resolving disagreements than by submitting them to the judgment of some arbiter. Hence the plaintive rhetorical question: "Who is to decide?"

It might further be suggested that the person who asks this question in this urgent way has never learned any way of deliberating about moral questions, and never doubts that they are matters to be settled by authority. It is altogether to be expected that there should be people like this. When we are very young, our parents and teachers do not tell us how to think about these things, but only what to do and what not to do. Learning to decide for ourselves is too difficult at that age, and is left for laters years. We accept various injunctions and prohibitions on the authority of our elders, and in that way it comes to seem to us that these are matters to be settled by authority. It is a shock to us when, in due course, we find that other people challenge the authorities we have trusted, and we set out in a fruitless search for some unchallengeable authority. The transition from being guided by an inherited set of injunctions and prohibitions to being able to decide for ourselves is not easily made. It involves a reorientation of our thinking in which what had been fundamental becomes derivative, and in which a set of certainties is replaced by the anxiety of reliance on one's own judgment. Moreover, while thinking for oneself is not profoundly difficult to learn, instruction in it is not often available. Most of us have to find out for ourselves how to do it, and we can make some bad mistakes along the way. Hence there are few people who can practise this art with skill and aplomb, and we are not familiar on an everyday basis with an abundance of clear and effective examples of it. Were it otherwise, it would be immediately obvious to us how absurd it is to ask, in that desperate, searching way, "Who is to decide?"

The foregoing is meant only as an illustration of how an overriding perplexity about the moral scene can be dismantled. It is to be noted that whereas I might most naturally have accepted the question, who is to decide? and set about answering it, instead I have mounted an argument that it is a mistake to press the question.

That kind of shift will be characteristic of the approach taken to the various perplexities in Chapter 5. Not every philosophical problem can be taken care of in this way, but it is a measure always worth trying because, as well as its elegance, it will in general have the outstanding advantage that whereas, if we attempt to answer this kind of question, we will be constructing theories that may often need to be quite elaborate and will be correspondingly controversial, nothing theoretical is generally involved in challenging the asking of the question. We do this by reiterating and making clear certain things with which we are already familiar. We all know, for example, that the question whether a certain action is morally recommendable is not a question of who advocates it and their credentials, but of whether anyone has a right to its performance, whether it would do any harm, whether such harm as might result is offset by benefits that would ensue, whether the persons suffering the harm are different from those enjoying the benefits, and so on.

In reading Chapters 1 to 4, it will be important to recognize and accept the distinction between the "ground-level" deliberations and the perplexities that can arise, not about their detail, but about the general manner in which they are conducted. It is not possible at the same time to discuss a question, and to discuss its discussability, or to discuss it and at the same time discuss the soundness of the way it is being discussed. Hence these two issues will resolutely be kept separate.

In the ground-level argumentation, it will be assumed that any objections will allege that a way of thinking about these matters which itself is quite in order has been bungled: facts have been overlooked or misrepresented, relevant distinctions have not been made, or fallacies have been committed. That is not to say that the more theoretical objections, concerning the overall way in which the "ground-level" deliberations are conducted, are disallowed. They are merely kept separate, to be considered in the final chapter.

It will be assumed throughout that, to put it one way, moral judgments make sense. What is meant by that is that one can be mistaken, or can get it right, as to what is a good thing to do or a bad thing, as to what one has a right or no right to do, as to what one has a duty to do, or not to do, and so on. Not many people doubt this, but some do, and anyone who does may feel that in Chapters 1 to 4 prior questions are blandly ignored at every turn.

The question whether moral judgments "make sense" is itself rationally discussable, but only confusion results from mixing the discussion of it with the discussion of particular moral issues. It is like trying to teach someone the fine points of a game, when the question bothering him is whether the game is worth playing. He will have difficulty taking much interest in the strategy and tactics of the game until his doubt is removed or he is persuaded to set it aside for the time being. One can discuss either his problem, or problems he will encounter if he plays, but not both at the same time.

The analogy can perhaps be exploited further: just as one of the best ways of deciding whether a game is worth playing is learning to play it at least moderately well, and only then deciding whether it is a rewarding activity, so it may be that one of the best ways of resolving scepticism as to whether moral judgments "make sense" is through learning a way of deciding moral questions, and only then coming to a conclusion as to whether one wishes to have any part of it. For one thing, it can hardly be clear otherwise just what one is rejecting, if one takes a sceptical stand with regard to the whole business. It may turn out, for example, that one has had a legitimate objection to some primitive, narrow or counter-productive forms of moral thinking, and that the objection is in fact shared by people who are not in the least sceptical as to whether moral judgments "make sense."

Perhaps few people will have these overriding doubts, but anyone who is troubled by them may be well advised, once having sampled at least enough of the ground-level discussion to know what method of transacting this business is being defended, to read Chapter 5 before proceeding further. It may not be found perfectly convincing, but will at least reassure the reader that the more abstract questions about moral thinking have not been overlooked.

ONE

Why Does Sex Seem So Important?

Sex occupies the thoughts of most human beings more of the time, and far more urgently, than any other single interest. It will be the business of this chapter to inquire just why this is so. Answering that question should not only prove intrinsically interesting, making an important contribution to our understanding of ourselves, but should help us to estimate how far sex deserves the importance we attach to it.

Does sex loom so large simply because it is so pleasant? Pleasures, no matter how intense or sublime, do not normally gain such a hold on the imagination that we crave them night and day and sometimes cannot turn our minds to other things because of them. Rather, we amuse ourselves languidly with the thought of pleasant things, and while we may jump at a chance to enjoy them, when they are unavailable we quite cheerfully direct our attentions elsewhere. If there were a wine whose taste and aroma we all found inexpressibly pleasant, then while it would be a matter of some concern how much of it there was, or how available it was to everyone, it would not, just because of its pleasantness, command our attention so very much more than other interests; and it would be a disaster from which the human race would very soon recover if one day this glorious stuff became unavailable.

Not so with making love. Although it is uncommonly pleasant, it is not out of all proportion more delightful than having an amusing conversation with a friend, eating a well-cooked meal, or anything else we very much enjoy; and yet it not only interests most of us more than any other of life's joys, but to be deprived of it bothers us to a degree unknown when we are deprived of other pleasures. Why is this?

It might be partly because sex gratifies us in more diverse ways than most other things we enjoy. It is often thought of as a physical pleasure—a "pleasure of the flesh," in some kinds of moral tract—and of course it is. There is nothing very intellectual about it. If we discussed philosophy or listened to music while making love, that would not make sex an intellectual or an aesthetic experience. We would simply be doing two things at the same time.

Yet the intellectual, aesthetic and the physical do not exhaust the kinds of pleasure there are; and making love, though not intellectual, is not just a physical experience. We rejoice not only in its tactile sensations, but in being in a euphoric state quite unlike our normal condition, in being so unrestrainedly demonstrative, in having our attention completely focused on and returned by someone we care for, in giving pleasure that shows so immediately and tangibly, in being able to express our attraction to another human being in such a sustained and concrete way, and in having that person accept and demonstrably exult in our interest. Although these delights would be nothing without the pleasures of touch with which they are entwined, they are not themselves physical pleasures.

However, even if the many emotional rewards of sexual activity contribute to explaining the enormous interest it commands, there must certainly be other contributing factors, because we do not all equally appreciate all of the features of lovemaking just described, nor do we always experience those pleasures when we make love, yet the intensity of our interest in sex remains high.

There are at least two other sorts of difference between our interest in making love and our interest in most other pleasant things. The first and most important is that our biological constitution predisposes us to sexual yearnings in a way that we are not predisposed to want to travel, sing madrigals or ride roller-coasters. Whereas we have no interest in most other activities apart from having tried and enjoyed them, we are keenly interested in sex prior to any experience of it, and would probably remain interested even if we found it a painful or distasteful experience.

Our thoughts do not wander urgently and at unexpected moments to the prospect of other pleasures, and we do not wake up in the night aching with a desire for them; but we do find ourselves quite taken over, sometimes against our better judgment, by sexual longings. In this, though not in other ways, sex resembles an addiction. We can want very much to smoke even when we have "been doing it more and enjoying it less." At such times we are driven to something quite independently of the pleasure it will yield. Similarly we seem to want sex in such a way that it can seem a nice bit of luck that it is so pleasant.

The fact that, whether we like it or not, we are passionate is the main contributor to the importance of sex. We are not all equally interested, but when anyone does burn with passion, no amount of self-discipline will greatly alter that fact. Prisoners, priests, nuns or people trying to live according to what we call the monogamous principle can find the stubborn insistency of their sexual yearnings profoundly regrettable, and some may even be able to achieve a measure of peace in various ways, but most often their resistance will be a perpetual struggle.

To have this passion thwarted by moral or other constraints on lovemaking is certainly disagreeable, and there is also much evidence of harmful psychological and social effects accruing from the repression of sexual longings. The danger here may sometimes be exaggerated, however. If it undeniably does happen that people's lives are distorted by sexual repression, that does not itself show that this consequence will inevitably, or even most likely, ensue; and in fact there are very large numbers of people who live through most of their passionate years without sexual experience and without obvious ill effect.

If it is argued that, because of the undesirable consequences of constraints on sexual activity, the constraints should be relaxed, the question is as much one of how good the reasons for the restrictions are, as one of how serious and widespread are the consequences. If the reasons were sufficiently strong, (a) we might work out ways of limiting the undesirable consequences, and (b) such consequences as remained notwithstanding such measures might have to be accepted as the price of achieving an important purpose.

In Chapters 2 and 3, we will be examining reasons for restricting sexual activity. The present point is only that these reasons do need to be considered when discussing the claim that the undesirable consequences of sexual repression show that we should be more liberal in our sexual attitudes.

We could distinguish between the conclusions policy makers might reach as to whether to arrange things so that more people could more often engage in sexual activity, and the deliberations of individuals about the conduct of their own affairs. For a person to make love, or make love more often, as a kind of preventive medicine — just out of fear that otherwise some dreadful psychological affliction would set in — would be an absurdly calculating motivation, and contrary to the enthusiastic and affectionate spirit of lovemaking. If the project of making love were broached in this way: "I have been concerned about the effects on my mental health of living a life without sex, and you too should be concerned about this, so I wonder if we might . . .", it would be a rare person who would consent for these reasons. However, this is the way it ought properly to be approached if concern for one's health were the real motivation.

There is something similarly unsatisfactory about justifying extramarital affairs by saying that it is "against human nature" to limit oneself to one person. We all know that marriage rarely puts an end to anyone's sexual enthusiasm and curiosity, but that is not the issue. The issue is whether it is nevertheless desirable to have a monogamous system; and that question is not settled just by pointing out a disadvantage that will hardly not have been noticed.

We have been dwelling on the fact that most of us are passionate. Since we all find passion troublesome at times, it may be interesting to consider how we would react if there were a pill we could take, or a gadget we could have installed, that would enable us to turn passion on and off at will. Suppose we found that while this pill or gadget provided welcome relief from unsatisfied sexual yearnings, it also had a number of other effects. People who had seemed beautiful or delightful would now seem uninteresting; love stories would be incomprehensible and dull; we would no longer devote energy to making ourselves personally attractive or to the cultivation of friendships involving a sexual interest, or if we did, we would do so coldly and without enthusiasm. We would feel no inclination to turn our passions back on, and if other people found ways of turning us on, we would feel annoyed with them for exercising this power over us. Although passion might return all right, it would now seem no longer to be *our* passion. We might feel as if we were in a hypnotic trance.

The imaginary pill may seem to offer the best of both worlds — enjoying sexuality on occasions of our choice, while not suffering the agony of unrelieved passion in between times. But few of us, if we clearly understood the differences it would make, would take this pill, at least not if its effects were permanent. We would prefer to bear with the agony of passion rather than lose all that we would be giving up in return for being free of it. Quite apart from any actual sexual activity on our part, it means a great deal to us to be, so to speak, members of the sexual community — to be interested in other people as sexual beings, to share imaginatively in the joys and hopes and fears of human sexuality, and to be players, if rarely stars, on that stage ourselves. It is probably true that these things are important to us only because we *are* passionate beings, and that what we would lose while under the influence of the imagined pill would not be missed. But it is equally true that a great deal of excitement would vanish from our lives.

We have been considering why it is that sex, though not incomparably more pleasant than some other activities, commands our interest so much more persistently. One reason is that we are passionate beings, driven to sex independently of its pleasantness; but there is much more than this contributing to our interest. Sometimes for good reason and sometimes for reasons that are not so good, we attach various kinds of significance to sexual activity. It seems to us to show various things, and we want it often less in itself than for what it shows.

In our culture, one thing that making love is often taken to show is solidarity with another person. It is taken as a demonstration of admiration, trust and affection. We want both to display these attitudes to another person and to have them displayed in return; and if there were something else that many people would do only as an expression of personal solidarity, such as joining with another person in a mystical rite, we would yearn to participate in that ceremony independently of any pleasures the rite might itself afford. Suppose that there were incense and music and wine of a uniquely delightful kind used in the ceremony, so that it could be wanted for its own sake and not for its significance. It might then be clearer that there are two quite distinct desires at work, one for the ceremony itself and the other for the unity with another person that it symbolizes.

By and large we do not attach this kind of significance to other pleasant activities involving other persons. We may prefer to play chess or tennis with someone who is funny or friendly or wise, but all that really matters is that the other person should play a good game; and we do not regard our playing with someone as having created any bond between us. Some people do treat sexual participation in very much the way they treat any other pleasure involving another person; and we can imagine a world in which everyone did, a world in which any partner would suffice, no significance attached to the fact that a person played, or played with a given partner, and in which the sole object was to have a satisfying engagement, and neither person felt that a bond was established by the fact of having played. Such a world might in some ways be a very much better one than the world as we know it; but as things stand a person has to be quite unusual and sophisticated, not only to sustain such an attitude against the powerful pressures militating against it, but to find sexual partners who genuinely share it. For no matter how liberated a person may aspire to be about sex, it is extremely difficult to check the emotional entanglements that arise from it, for whatever cultural or psychological reasons.

One may be inclined to regard the fact that in our culture this kind of significance attaches to sexual activitiy as artificial and unnecessary; and of course it is. It might very well have been otherwise, and we might, if we went about it strenuously, change all the customs and practices that make us think of sex that way. The question, however, is not whether it is artificial, but whether it is a good thing; and the answer to that question is that it is good in many ways, but also has undesirable aspects.

The undesirable aspects of the emotional significance of sexual activity are that it makes it more difficult to achieve sexual satisfaction, that it creates possibilities of deception and misunderstanding that would not otherwise exist, that it often ties people together who are ill suited to one another, and that it frequently leads to bitterness and heartbreak when lovers prove false. If we were as unromantic about sex as we are about eating, not only might we have more of it and enjoy it more, but there would be little or no place for the tensions, contrivances, jealousies and bitterness that now often surround it.

On the other hand, when we regard making love as demonstrating personal solidarity, something splendid can come to pass that would not be possible under less romantic auspices, namely the exultation that two people will find in making love when each knows that the other would not do it if he were not in love and the utter confidence in their good relationship that the lovemaking demonstrates. One can live without these rewards, certainly, and the complex of attitudes that makes them possible is bought at some price, as we saw and will see further; nevertheless life would be poorer without them.

Even for people who do not care to see sexual activity as a celebration of personal solidarity, or as anything more than a very special kind of pleasure, there are forces at work that can make it extremely difficult for them to free themselves entirely from such romantic conceptions. One of these is that from a very early age we are sedulously conditioned to guard our bodily privacy, and to discourage bodily contact beyond the handshake. Even if it were not spelled out to us, it would naturally come to seem that the relaxation of the bodily privacy barrier should be reserved for quite special circumstances. There is, of course, more than one possibility as to what these circumstances had best be, but one obvious possibility is that the existence of a mutual attraction and trust between two people should be a condition for relaxing the barrier.

Secondly, it is not entirely conventional that the physical closeness that is such a prominent feature of sexual activity should symbolize personal closeness. We see little children, who are not yet acquainted with such conventions, holding hands and huddling together when they are lost or afraid; and when we kiss or embrace another person, neither the tactile pleasure nor the conventional significance (nor the two together) sufficiently explains the satisfaction derived. The tactile pleasure is slight, and we can imagine other conventions having existed that did not involve touching and holding, were it not that nothing is so real to us as when we touch it. When we are enthusiastic about another person, although it may be their gentleness, courage, wit or wisdom that pleases us, still we want to touch and hold the possessor of those qualities, because nothing gives us a stronger sense of union and reality.

Thirdly, other people tend to *make* one play the role of good friend, by demanding admiration and concern before they will consider making love. While there are some people cynical or disingenuous enough to pretend, and skilful enough to do so successfully, an average person will find such pretense distasteful, and so will decline the role except when it can be played in good faith. In this way one can come to accept a romantic conception simply as the only way one can function honestly in prevailing conditions.

These pressures to see lovemaking as an expression of personal solidarity are of course not inexorable, but they are present, and they are likely to affect even the person who resists them, and to result in lingering dissatisfaction with sexual activity undertaken purely for pleasure. And even those who manage completely to overcome them may still have difficulty linking up with others who have achieved the same level of liberation or disenchantment.

There are other ways in which we attach significance to sexual activity, and want it as much for its significance as for its own sake. Most of these ways, it will be seen, while they do contribute to the importance attaching to sex, have much less tendency to show that it deserves to be so important.

There are in the first place some offshoots of the fact that so many people attach significance to having made love that can contribute to our desire for it. One may want to make love to a person one admires, in part because it would prove that there was a good personal relationship, that the admiration and acceptance were altogether mutual.

It is a little difficult to distinguish this case from that in which two people want to make love as much for what it symbolizes as for the pleasure of it. The difference is that in the latter case there are no doubts, and nothing stands to be proven. Contrast the case in which two people enjoy and admire one another, and are exultant when one day they make love, with the case in which, although there is an amicable enough relationship, and one person is intensely interested, it is not clear to this person whether the interest is mutual, or runs very deep. Perhaps there are slight awkwardnesses in the friendship. Conversations about some topics are strained. There is rather too much need to work at entertaining the other person. Or perhaps it is not that so much, as that the other person is just as affable with, and apparently interested in, any number of other people. Hence there are doubts as to whether the relationship is more than merely amicable, or perhaps exploratory. It may then seem that these doubts would surely be removed if the two were to do something so intimate and symbolic as to make love.

One can want most intensely to remove doubts as to the depth of the other person's feeling, and want to make love at least as much as a way of achieving this as for the joy of it. Yet in an average case such a project is ill conceived. It is like wishing one were brave, and wanting a medal to satisfy that wish; or perhaps better, it is like having done something not clearly courageous, and feeling that a medal would settle doubts as to whether it was brave.

If Peter admires Alison and they see a good deal of one another and enjoy doing things together, but she never seems to him to reveal herself, and there is just nothing that shows whether she cares particularly about him, those facts themselves show that the relationship is less than ideal. If perhaps he says how much he admires her, and she is glad of it, but still does not respond with anything that shows whether it is mutual; or if she does say something affectionate, but he is unsure whether to believe it, something is not working well between them. It may not matter whether this is because she somehow fails to make her feelings clear, or because he requires too much convincing. There is something not working; and there is little reason to expect that things will be different in this regard if they make love. It may still be unclear whether she made love out of fondness for him, or just because she enjoys sex, as she has enjoyed other things they have done together.

It is not that these questions can never be settled. It is often perfectly clear how another person feels, and when there is room for doubt, the doubt can often soon be removed. A friend may say, "How can you be in any doubt about her enthusiasm for you? Haven't you noticed how particularly animated she is when she is with you? And why do you suppose she goes to political rallies and boxing matches? She never did anything like that before." And so on. Or the doubt may be removed by a heart-to-heart talk. The point is that, if there is indeed something unsatisfactory about the relationship, it cannot be proven that things are otherwise; while if the relationship only seems less than ideal, perhaps because of the undemonstrativeness of the persons involved, its fundamental soundness can be brought out in ways more accessible and more convincing than by making love.

It is perhaps possible to hope, not that making love would prove something, but that through it a relationship might be improved. One might imagine that barriers would be broken down, and that a new and special feeling would come to exist between people who had done such a singular thing together.

It could happen that two people make love, not for this reason, but just because sex is so pleasant, and find to their delight that things start to go much better between them in other ways. Whether this happened would perhaps depend on the ways in which their relationship had been unsatisfactory. If they were badly mismatched, and perhaps attracted only by such things as physical beauty or local fame, it is likely that when they became lovers, the discrepancy between the physical intimacy and the strained character of their relationship generally would seem bizarre, and accentuate rather than relieve the strain. On the other hand, if the main awkwardness had been due to bashfulness or lack of self-confidence, it is likely this would be removed by their making love, and possible that their relationship would then flower.

Yet while in such a case this might be the happy consequence, we imagine it accruing as a delightful surprise, and not as being the end in view. Clearly it would be altogether different if the would-be lovers were to embark on it deliberately, to achieve this end; for example, if one of them said one day, "Look, we get on quite well in many ways, but things are strained between us often, and I think it is entirely due to diffidence on both our parts. But if we were to make love, we could hardly be shy of one another any longer, and we'd say and do many things that up to now we have hesitated to do. So what do you say? Should we try that?" If this tactic worked, it would be one of the most remarkable seductions that has ever occurred; however, the chances of its succeeding in its aim are not great, because it is too contrived. Making love may break down some barriers when it occurs spontaneously, but hardly when one is watching anxiously for the benefits to accrue, if only because a person would have to be unusually calculating to set about it in this way.

Sexual success can appear to us also as a demonstration of our charms, or of our masculinity or femininity. Not everyone who leads a busy sex life does so out of personal vanity. Some storybook characters, like Fielding's Tom Jones, just enjoy other people, and have an uncommon zest for making love; but anyone who pursues the project of an active sex life with a kind of relentlessness, talks boastfully about it, takes a special interest in anyone who appears as a challenge, or is disturbed by failures, is likely trying to prove something.

For many people, this attitude need only be described to be discredited; but perhaps not for the person who *has* it. So let us set aside our distaste for the vanity of it, and for its tendency to use other people merely as a means of proving something, and ask what in fact is proved in this way?

If one wanted to demonstrate one's sexual attractiveness, while one seduction might not do the job, half a dozen surely would, at least if the partners involved were persons of some discrimination who would not accept just anyone who displayed some enthusiasm for them. Thereafter the point would be established, and to go on and on making it would prove nothing so much as an insecurity on this person's part. However, not everyone who has this need for constant reassurance confines the pursuit of it to really challenging projects — people who are not easily seduced, with whom success might therefore demonstrate something — and since large numbers of people are keen for sex partners, an active sex life may demonstrate only an ability to spot an easy conquest. A person who is not sexually attractive cannot prove otherwise, even through elaborate sexual derring-do; while if one is attractive, that fact will generally be clear enough just from the kind of interest other people show.

A rather different source of our interest in sex is the storybook quality it acquires from films, novels, advertising and everyday chitchat, a quality accentuated by the aura of forbiddenness that enhances this remarkable pleasure. Even people who do not themselves think sex wicked may savor the idea of doing something so widely felt to be sinful. A love affair can seem like a journey into a magic world of romance and high adventure.

Yet this illusion is hard to maintain in practice, and likely in the end to reduce, rather than enhance, the pleasure of making love. It may prove disappointing that, however joyful the event may be, the people we are, the things we say, the circumstances surrounding us seldom count as the material of which fables are made.

In this chapter we have depicted some of the genuinely marvellous things about sexual activity, while noting some of the ways in which we may want it too much, through having false expectations as to what it will mean, what it will prove, or how it will change our lives.

In our cultural climate, it is almost bound to happen that many people will have some or other of these false expectations. It is one question whether we might therefore try to change the climate, and another question whether, taking things as they are, individuals can at least hammer out for themselves an approach to their sexual lives that makes sex the delightful and meaningful thing it is capable of being, without exaggerating its charms or its importance.

The former project is likely at the very least to be too long-term an affair to do you or me any good, and is also likely to replace present attitudes with new ones themselves capable of distortion. The latter project has the merit of being within the reach at least of people with some capacity for going their own way. Whatever attitude anyone comes to have, there will be no way of avoiding all friction with people of a different cast of mind, but a thoughtful attitude, having some depth, can be pursued with poise and without rancor; and it may not be too optimistic to hope that one may find at least some people who can share it.

It is not suggested that one must choose between these two "projects." Clearly one could pursue both; but working something out for oneself is both available and urgent. In any case, without undertaking this, one is unlikely to succeed in affecting the cultural climate generally.

TWO

What Are the Moral Issues in Our Sex Lives?

In our culture, it is difficult to avoid taking some stand or another on the ethics of any number of forms of human activity. We do something and are told it is wrong, hesitate to do something and are told it is our duty, consider doing something and are advised that although it would be a good thing to do, we are not under any obligation to do it, and so on. We constantly have to take some stand on questions like this.

Sexual behavior, although it is by no means the only topic of such allegations, is both one with which a very large number of them are concerned, and one about which the allegations are made with a particular urgency. Some sophisticated people shrug off moral claims of any kind, saying such things as that they do not know what the words in which the claims are expressed mean, or that they can only regard them as expressions of a peculiar kind of personal distaste or of personal favor, and that they do not see themselves as bound in any way to gratify these prejudices.

Over the centuries, a great deal of philosophical energy has been devoted to the questions thereby raised. These are not questions as to which actions we can be morally required to do or avoid, or which actions it is morally preferable to do or avoid, but as to whether perhaps the whole business of trying to require or forbid various forms of behavior is a human aberration.

Those questions are profoundly difficult, and it is not clear whether philosophical efforts to solve them have so far been rewarded with any success. Two examples of the many peculiar difficulties that arise are:

1. It is difficult even to state the problem without either presupposing, or leaving it unclear whether one has presupposed, part of what is presumed to be at issue. If a person expresses a doubt as to whether he is "bound to gratify these prejudices," is the word "bound" a moral word, and can he mean anything by it if he is sceptical as to whether moral words mean anything? Again, if one puts it that "perhaps the whole business is a human aberration," does that not mean that it would be "better" if we were to cease and desist from it? And is "better," as here used, a moral word?

2. Suppose someone says that to shrug off morals is itself to take a moral stand: that one is "entitled" to disregard these claims. It is not clear that this is true, and the radical sceptic would of course want to deny it; but how is it to be decided? It is not enough for the sceptic to say that he does not claim a right, he is just enunciating an attitude. If he is not in some sense claiming entitlement to his attitude, it is queer that he should be arguing about it, rather than just declaring it. He might say that his entitlement is of some nonmoral kind, but how can he substantiate the claim, if not by saying, "Moral entitlement is thus and so, and this entitlement is clearly different, and neither thus or so." He cannot say this, however, because he does not allow that there is a concept of moral entitlement.

For good or ill, the human race has not waited for philosophers to settle these maddening prior questions, before carrying on with the practice of requiring or encouraging people to do or avoid various things, and of deliberating as to which things to require or encourage.

There has never been a widely accepted method of settling these questions, and certainly not one which, if carefully followed, would produce an answer in every case, or even in most cases. Nor were any methods that did exist taught as methods. No one said, "This is the way we decide a moral question: we do thus and so, and then such and such," and no one drilled students in the technique until they could operate it competently. People *have* learned something about moral deliberation, but they have learned it chiefly from listening in on the arguments that occur and participating in them. Because these arguments are not always well conducted, different people have learned different things. Also, because the techniques of argument are rarely described, people remain unclear as to what they have learned. They can do something, but cannot say how it is done — just as a self-taught skier may regularly execute a fine stem-christie, without at all being able to explain how to do it.

The point of all this is that whether we like it or not, by the time most of us are confronted with any serious moral decisions, we are already initiates in the practice of moral deliberation. We may not be very good at it, and we may have acquired some unusual ways of going about it, but if what we do is to be called moral deliberation, it can hardly be entirely different from what other people do.

The equipment we have acquired for thinking about moral questions is all we have to work with. With it we can challenge any particular moral claim, but it can hardly be used to bring itself in question. Whatever our mode of moral deliberation may be, it will be a way of deciding as to the ethics of this and that, and not a way of deciding whether the decisions taken in accordance with the technique need to be taken seriously.

If I have been in the habit of thinking that any action that is disadvantageous to me is therefore virtuous, that is part of my technique for deciding various questions. It may itself be brought in question; for example, if I reflect that very often no one benefits by these self-denying actions of mine. In this, however, I am questioning a part, and not the whole of my way of thinking. The part that is not currently in question gives me a basis on which to reason; but if I question the whole of my way of thinking, I have no ground left on which to stand. I can say, "To hell with the whole business. I'll do what I please," but I am logically prevented from adducing any justification for this stand.

This way of looking at it provides an explanation of the peculiar difficulties we saw arising when one attempts to question the whole business of moral thinking. Either moral concepts creep in, sometimes in artful disguises, or one is left with no grounds for the stand one is attempting to take.

It also provides one way of defending the general position that will be adopted in these deliberations, namely that while no specific point of morals can be treated as unchallengeable, radical scepticism is ruled out, that is to say no doubt will be allowed as to whether there is *some* answer to most moral questions.

Probably not many people worry as to whether this at least is true, or even ask themselves this question. In practice we are not concerned as to whether some things are right, wrong, better, worse, and so on, but we are often quite uncertain as to *which* things are so; and that is the kind of question with which we will be dealing here.

The basic test that will be employed in answering these questions is that of asking whether an action is dishonest, unfair, cruel, selfish, cowardly or dangerous. We will take it that if an action has any of these properties, it is so far not morally recommendable. If it has the opposite of one or more of them, it is so far morally desirable; and if it has a mixed bag of good and bad features, its evaluation consists of a fair statement of its merits and faults.

This is a crude instrument, and will not always provide us with uncontroversial answers to moral questions. For one thing, there can be disagreement as to whether an action is unfair or cowardly, and in some cases perhaps even as to whether it is dishonest, cruel or dangerous. For another, it is not claimed that the list of qualities given is exhaustive, and it is not clear how we would decide whether other features, such as being blasphemous or unfriendly, should be included in the list. Thirdly, it may often be unclear how to rate the relative importance of the merits and faults of an action; for example, if some important purpose is served by it, but at some cost to a person who cannot fairly be asked to bear this cost. Yet however unsatisfactory this crude instrument may be, it is all we have to work with, and we must make of it what we can.

Crude instruments are better than none at all, and in fact we can do a great deal with what we have. People dwell and harp on the difficulties that can arise in special cases, and forget that these cases are comparatively rare, and that often there is no controversy as to whether, for example, an action is dishonest or unfair.

Again, although certainly it will remain a possibility that an action has a merit or a fault not considered in some initial evaluation of it, still an argument to the effect that an action is neither dishonest, unfair, cruel or cowardly does show something about it, and need not preclude anyone from pointing out some other, perhaps less familiar, fault. If it were accepted that to act in haste was a moral fault, but not one that loomed large in our thinking, our initial evaluation might rarely consider this possibility, but there would still always be room for the rejoinder, "Yes, but it was done in haste." Although this would make a difference, it would not affect the truth and importance of the fact that the action was neither dishonest, unfair nor cruel.

Thirdly, when an action has some merits and some faults, and there seems no way of balancing these to yield a clear recommendation, then in default of further insight that is itself the moral truth about that action. If anyone asks, "Then how do I know whether to do it?", the answer is that, in view of its faults, if you do it you will not be blameless, while in view of its merits, doing it will not be unqualifiedly wrong. Perhaps it is then a question of what alternatives are available; but if, as sometimes happens, it is that or nothing, we may sometimes have to live with the idea that whatever we do will have its regrettable aspects.

WHEN IS MAKING LOVE IMMORAL?

Having described a method of answering moral questions, let us now apply it to some problems having to do with our sex lives.

In this section, we will proceed as if the monogamous principle, which until recently was the official sexual morality of North

America and most of Europe, did not exist, or as if we had never heard of it. This is the principle that sexual activity is morally acceptable only within the bounds of marriage. The merits of that principle will be discussed in the following section, but for the present our question will be what, apart from any claims it makes upon us, are the main circumstances in which sexual activity can be morally acceptable or otherwise.

One could easily get the impression in our culture that sexual activity is widely believed to be inherently sinful—even when it is embarked upon under approved auspices such as marriage, or for the specific purpose of begetting children — and that, whatever they say to the contrary, many people think that in an ideal world children would either be created in some other way, or human beings would be so constituted as to find the age-old way a necessary chore to be undertaken with genuine distaste.

Not many adults would now confess to having such an attitude, or anything resembling it, yet it is not difficult to see how a young person might come to suppose that this was the attitude of most parents, schoolteachers and clergymen. There are so many ways in which we seem to treat sex as dirty or naughty, and as a kind of undercurrent of our lives, a secret obsession that you might never guess we had if you observed only our public behavior. We guard our bodily privacy, we are slightly alarmed at physical contact, we conduct our sexual activities in the deepest seclusion, we are shy about describing or discussing them, we are alarmed at the thought of what our children may be up to sexually, and we are both fascinated and repelled by any explicit depiction of love-making on the stage or in films.

From such pervasive features of our culture, and many others of the same kind, a person can without realizing it absorb the notion of the sinfulness of sex: it seeps into one's consciousness, not as an explicit conviction, but as a very basic attitude, determining one's responses to such things as books, films, jokes and what we learn or surmise about the sex lives of other people. Yet when the ingrained attitude is given explicit expression as a moral theorem, it quite clearly fails the known tests of moral defect: making love is neither always nor typically cruel, harmful, deceitful, unfair, selfish or cowardly, and hence is at least not inherently sinful.

It is true that there may be selfishness, cruelty or deception involved in a sexual relationship, and when that is true, of course there is something morally defective about it; but making love neither need involve any such moral fault, nor are such faults so difficult to avoid in our sex lives as to make it rare for sexual activity to be morally blameless. If it rarely happened that one could make love without deception or serious risk of harm, there might be a case for saying that, although not necessarily wrong, it is best avoided because of the very high moral risk; but given elementary candor and discretion, it is not difficult to achieve a relationship in which there is no serious prospect of deception, suffering or heartbreak. Such relationships happen all the time.

A person who, having been culturally encouraged to believe that sex is inherently shameful, later comes, by some such reasoning as we have described, to see that it is not may easily make the mistake of thinking that in this he is disagreeing with most members of the adult world. It was from their attitudes and reactions that he acquired his impression of the immorality of sex, so can he not reasonably take it that they believe what he has now rejected?

Such reasoning may be an important ingredient in the generation gap, and is therefore worth examining with some care. Much will depend here on whether there are other explanations of the adult behavior that has generated the impression of the sinfulness of sex. In the first place, if the impression has been generated in part by explicit declarations, these may have been a kind of overstatement to which we are often tempted or driven. Here, because it is less controversial, we could use the example of a parent teaching a child about lying. The parent, we will suppose, has a complicated attitude towards truthfulness, believing that it is sometimes a duty to lie in order to achieve some more important end, but there are some cases in which other ends must be sacrificed, because it is more important that a person know the truth, even if it will pain him. The parent hesitates, however, to confuse the child with such complex considerations, and believing that for the time being the child will not go far wrong if he always tells the truth, says categorically that lying is wrong. Since the child cannot be assumed to know what is meant by the word "wrong," the parent may accompany the teaching with gestures of horror and distaste. The child comes away from this with the false, but understandable, impression that the parent is an absolutist about lying, and has an attitude toward any case of it not unlike our reaction to rancid meat. Some explicit teachings as to the sinfulness of sex may similarly be more categorical than the beliefs of the teachers themselves, and may be so in an effort to avoid confusing children at the outset with more complexities than are necessary for their current purposes.

Secondly, there are other explanations of many inexplicit indicators of moral attitudes towards sex. People hesitate to talk about their sex lives, not because they are ashamed, but for such reasons as that these are very personal matters, to be shared only between those directly involved. (People do not make love in public for much the same reason, as well as for more practical reasons.) Parents can be intensely concerned about the sex lives of their children, not because they think that any sexual activity on their part will be sinful, but because they know it can be difficult to achieve a mature understanding of these things, and that the attitude one adopts will likely have an important influence on the kind of person one becomes and the kind of relationships one seeks.

The argument so far is only that one cannot safely infer people's beliefs or attitudes either from their explicit teachings or from such items of behavior as hesitancy to talk about sex. Nothing we have said shows what anyone's attitude in fact is. The test of that would be what a person would say when the cards were down — that is, what would be said between equals who were articulate about their convictions and had no reason to fear or distrust one another.

Unfortunately perhaps, this test is seldom applied. One can only conjecture as to why not, but it may be because it is difficult to replace the initial authoritarian relationship between parent and child or teacher and pupil, as years go by, with one of equality. Even if equality is achieved, we are generally insufficiently articulate about sensitive questions and seldom feel that we have nothing to fear from a frank expression of moral opinion.

The practical upshot of these last reflections is perhaps that it is unsafe to make inferences as to people's moral convictions in any case except when they are talking to someone they conceive to be an equal and, with nothing to fear, are addressing themselves specifically to the project of accurately stating their views; and second, that since such conditions are rare, it is best not to have any view as to whether, in arriving at the conclusion that sex is not inherently sinful, one is taking a view that is new or revolutionary.

It is no great advance to find that sexual activity is not inherently sinful. At most it rids us of a doubt as to whether something we may suspect some people believe might be true. It might also help some of us to surmount something that, for confused psychological reasons, we half believe; but it shows nothing as to whether making love is sometimes wrong, and certainly nothing as to just when it is, if ever.

Since the advent of reliable methods of contraception, it has become possible to claim with at least some show of plausibility that as long as such contraceptives are used, making love heterosexually is never wrong. The argument would be that in the past the only legitimate source of moral concern was the risk of pregnancy, and now that this risk is removed, it is a matter of moral indifference when or with whom one makes love.

This contention would very clearly lack all plausibility without the provision that effective contraceptives be used, because although there no longer *need* be more than a somewhat remote risk of pregnancy, there remain powerful forces working against the unfailing use of contraceptives. Among these are the following:

- Young people especially, but others as well, may be embarrassed about consulting a doctor about contraceptives, or purchasing them.
- Young people living at home with parents who would disapprove may avoid owning contraceptives for fear of their discovery.
- In our culture, making love outside of marriage is for many people an act of moral abandon, and in the mood of abandon in which it is done, being so scrupulous as to use a contraceptive may be unusual.
- One of the roles in which a woman is cast requires her to resist a man's advances, and yield to him only at intensely romantic moments, and as a surprise even to herself. A woman who accepts this role wholeheartedly, and some do, cannot very well come equipped with a contraceptive, at least not the first time.
- People who live together, but make love only when, after some love play, they are sexually excited, may find that it breaks the spell they are in, to stop and do something so humdrum as making contraceptive arrangements.
- Some people have doubts as to whether some methods of contraception are harmful; and some people believe that the use of contraceptives is itself immoral.

In any of these cases, even given that the risk of pregnancy is the only moral issue, sexual activity can still be of very serious moral concern. Moreover, a finer question arises, inasmuch as birth control methods vary a great deal in efficiency, and the best of them, as some people know to their sorrow, cannot be absolutely counted on. Is one morally justified in running the risk, however small, of such an extremely undesirable thing as an unwanted pregnancy?

Here it is possible for serious people to disagree. On the one hand it can be argued that there is risk in most everything we do, and that to be over-fussy about risks when they are slight will unduly restrict the color and richness of life. There is a risk of drowning when we swim, and of grievous damage to persons and property when we drive cars, but no one advocates for these reasons that we give up these activities.

On the other hand, such risks are either to ourselves, or if to other people, are generally accepted. Even people who never travel by car themselves accept the risk to them that lies in other people's use of motor vehicles. However, no one can accept a risk on someone else's behalf, but that is what is involved when we run the risk of begetting an unwanted child.

If a man and woman made love with the attitude that although they did not wish to become parents they would, if a pregnancy resulted, nurture and care for the child, there would be no problem. However, not many people who make love outside of marriage have that attitude; and not all of those who do are sufficiently compatible to stay with the project if fate calls upon them to do so. (The question of the ethics of abortion also clearly has a place here. It is discussed in detail on pages 120–35.)

There is an ethical principle whose soundness is hard to challenge that has a bearing here; namely, that something having moral value cannot be weighed against something having none. If I cannot help one person without falling down on a duty to help another, I have a moral problem, because both options are morally valuable; but if there is something I want to do very much, although someone would suffer by my doing it, or if I am in a position to confer a considerable benefit, but I do not want to do it, then while it may be a problem for me what to do, it is not a problem of what it would be *morally* best to do. There may, it is true, be cases of this kind in which I can seriously claim a right to my personal preference, but those are again cases in which both of the options weighed have a moral value. Making love, at least in the case in which two people want to add sex to the ways in which they enjoy one another, is not a duty or a virtue, and therefore on the above principle, it is not something that can be weighed against any morally important interests of another human being.

Perhaps only the very scrupulous would be moved by these considerations into abstaining from making love just on account of the slight risk of pregnancy when using a superior method of contraception, but they have a serious and honest argument that commands respect. When the risk is genuinely slight it will be respectable to disagree, but only when it is slight; and as we have seen, even in this age of contraceptives, that is by no means always.

In any case the risk of pregnancy is fairly clearly not the only moral consideration in the conduct of our sex lives. To adopt that view without further deliberation or argument would in the first place be to undervalue what we called "the monogamous principle." That is not to say that this principle must be accepted, but only that it should not be rejected quite so summarily, and without careful consideration of its possible merits. In the second place, even apart from any moral problems stemming from the monogamous principle, there are quite clearly many ways in which the pursuit of our sexual ambitions can involve deception, grief and harm, not only to the persons with whom we make love, but very often to others.

In a world in which there was absolute control of the incidence of pregnancy, in which also venereal disease was unknown, and in which, except at the few times in their lives when people wanted to have a child, we got together sexually strictly for the fun of it, our sex lives might generate as few moral problems as do most other forms of recreation. If we made love as casually as we fall into conversation with strangers on a bus, and had no other thoughts about it afterwards than perhaps whether it was as pleasant this time as it sometimes is, there would be little or no room for the machinations, deceptions, jealousies and agonies that, as things stand, often surround our sex lives, and are due mainly to some of the attitudes that were described in Chapter 1.

Some people may think that such a world is desirable, and be impatient with the present widespread tendency to attach various kinds of significance to our sexual engagements, and as a consequence to generate misunderstandings, anxieties and disappointments. Thinking that this tendency is unnecessary and foolish, they may be inclined to discount the various moral considerations arising out of it, taking the view that although they are real enough, in an ideal world they would not arise.

For good or ill, wisely or foolishly, in the world as we know it, many people do attach various kinds of significance to sexual affairs. They reserve themselves for people they like or admire, treat sexual relations as a demonstration of love and trust, see them as establishing bonds between people of candor and continuing friendship. Not everyone shares all, or even any, of these attitudes, but there are some people who have them all, and many who have some of them; and wherever the attitudes exist, moral problems arise. Deception may have to be practiced in order to represent oneself as a suitable sexual partner; and heartbreak and bitterness can result when a partner proves not to have been so interested, so committed or so trustworthy as was required or as he or she appeared to be. Any serious person would have to regard these possibilities of deception and suffering as morally important.

There are other factors that, while they may likewise be, or seem to some people to be, unnecessary, still are real and make morally important differences. Some of us are unclear or ambivalent about sexual morals, and while we may, in the heat of passion or to please someone we love, set aside our doubts and make love, we may feel guilty about it, and cheapened by this indulgence in pleasure contrary to principles we half believe in. This torment of the soul is not only undesirable in itself, it can have serious consequences. It can diminish a person's self-esteem. In confused ways, people can come to regard themselves as morally inferior, as lacking some quality they fancy other people possess. Hence they come to require less of themselves, and to be less particular with whom they associate. In this and similar ways, undesirable effects can flow from a sense of guilt which, although it may be quite unnecessary, is nevertheless real.

A different sort of problem can arise from the fact that, in sexual affairs, we tangle with the moral convictions, not only of the participants themselves, but of friends, families, and the community. Two people who themselves see no moral objection to a sexual liaison may have close ties with people who would be appalled if they learned of such a turn of events. They may thereby be faced with a choice between painfully straining otherwise good relationships, or embarking on an elaborate practice of pretence and deception — either of which one would morally want to avoid.

In short, the risk of pregnancy is by no means the only way in which our sex lives can involve us in such prime moral faults as cruelty, deception, unfairness or selfishness.

It is an important fact about the various features we have just been noting that, unlike the risk of pregnancy, which is a biological fact, these features are all culturally determined and could, we may think, very well be otherwise. The morally ambivalent person who feels guilty about sexual activity even when it is not harmful or deceitful might very easily not have had those qualms; the parents or friends who are shocked might very easily have looked on the affair as something beautiful and most welcome; the person who treats lovemaking as establishing a bond and is bitter when it proves otherwise might well have looked on it simply as a form of pleasure; and so on. The attitudes in these cases do exist, and do lead to grief and deception; but anyone who thinks (a) that they are foolish or ill-founded, and (b) that they could, if only their defectiveness were perceived, be otherwise, is liable to think that in spite of their consequences they do not deserve to be taken seriously, or to enter the reckoning as to how a responsible person will behave.

It might simplify the discussion of this peculiarly puzzling problem if we set aside the question of whether these beliefs and attitudes are foolish or ill-founded, or could be otherwise. In any case in which we could show that they are wise and for the best, the precise problem we are now considering would not arise; but we all have to cope sometimes with attitudes that are fairly clearly unwise, or that we at any rate believe to be so. Hence to discuss the justifiability of any given attitude will not take us to the root of the matter, and we will do best to confine the discussion to cases in which, rightly or wrongly, we believe a troublesome attitude to be ill founded.

Two possible justifications can be suggested for ignoring undesirable consequences resulting from someone's having an unwise or unnecessary attitude. The first we might call the reformer's reason. When faced with what one believes to be human folly or moral backwardness, one may think that by acting in a way one would act if it did not exist, one will be contributing to its demise, either by displaying for the enlightenment of the unimaginative the merits of a new mode of conduct, or by making it uncomfortable for the misguided to continue in their beliefs, thereby generating a pressure to change. If Peter and Martha would like to become lovers, but their parents would be horrified and profoundly unhappy, the reformer's thought would be either that by going ahead with it and proving that something excellent can come to pass that way, or by showing the disapproving parents that their moral convictions only lead to their own and other people's unhappiness, a definite step would be taken towards a more liberal and enlightened world.

One may be suspicious of this line of justification because there is some duality of motivation. The lovers are not making love just as a way of altering the convictions of the people who will disapprove. Quite independently of that, they want to be lovers, and only when confronted with the prospect of other people's disappointment and sorrow do they bethink themselves of the general moral enlightenment that would result. Yet while that project might for some people be merely a rationalization, it is not impossible for people to do things for two distinct reasons, both of them quite genuine, and therefore we could not say that their justification was necessarily defective because of the duality of motivation. Whether it was defective would depend perhaps on how many and how intelligent were the steps they took specifically to drive home the moral point they wanted to make; for example, whether they were restrained in the face of bitterness and denunciation, whether they were at pains to make clear, not just that they were lovers, but the features of their relationship that might command respect and sympathy, and so on.

The hard question would be as to the possibility of success. It makes sense to risk causing considerable harm if one thereby stands a fairly good chance of achieving something desirable; but the smaller the chance of success the less defensible is running the risk of harm. Although I may disapprove of the practice of tipping, I can hardly suppose I am contributing to its abolition by not tipping myself. It is of course different in the case we are discussing, because in it one would be dealing only with the attitudes of a few people, whereas in the tipping case one is dealing with a very widespread practice. Yet in view of the intensity with which moral convictions about sex are held, in the average case there is really so little prospect of their being changed in the way we are imagining, that this line of justification must on the whole be rejected. That is not to say that there may not be special cases in which it would have some merit.

The other possible justification for ignoring the ill consequences flowing in these cases from convictions or attitudes believed to be defective is that to do otherwise would have too conservative a tendency: one would then have to respect the wishes of anyone, no matter how unenlightened, whenever by not doing so grief and hard feelings would result or an otherwise good personal relationship would be spoiled.

Here it is of some importance that the conservative tendency could easily be exaggerated: one would not have to defer to every and any unenlightened attitude. I may disapprove of the actions of someone I scarcely know, but since there is no good relationship between us to be destroyed, and since I am hardly likely to grieve over his actions, the fact of my disapproval creates no moral problem for him. It is only between closely related persons that the conservative principle would operate. Even so, its effect would be far from negligible.

Moreover, the conservative principle, in the cases where it operates, may only serve to delay the achievement of something we think desirable, or to require that it be achieved in some other way, because often there are other alternatives, even if they are not easily achieved, or always available.

One of these we might call the picking and choosing alternative: confining one's sexual friendships to persons who are not morally ambivalent, or do not attach a significance to sexual activities that will result in bitterness or disillusionment, or whose friends or family will not have to be deceived about the affair. This alternative will sound easy and sensible until one is confronted with the fact that one is interested in a specific person who has some of these liabilities, and that no one else will do as a substitute.

A second approach might be called the patience and persuasion alternative. If your friend is morally ambivalent, talk out the morality of it, and wait until it seems that the ambivalence has cleared up; if your friend attaches a significance to sex that you cannot accept, explain your attitude and try to show it is one that a self-respecting person could hold; if relations with family or friends would be strained, make clear to them what your views are about sexual morality, in the hope that they may at least come to see that such views can be responsibly held and that it is a matter about which people can respectfully disagree.

However good the patience and persuasion approach may sound on paper, it is difficult in practice, for any number of reasons. It is awkward to talk about sexual morality with someone who may be personally involved in the outcome of the discussion, because of the difficulty of removing the suspicion of special pleading, the suspicion that any point you make is made less because of its inherent soundness than because it may get you what you want. It also seems to many people contrary to the nature of lovemaking to talk about it and reach a rational understanding beforehand. Discussion seems to destroy the romance and magic of doing this odd and wonderful thing, which seems properly to be done out of the intensity of one's feeling. Moreover, since emotions about sexual morality run so deep, few of us are adept at discussing the subject. We become rattled and say silly things, which lead to sillier things; and before long communication has broken down. And just because we feel so deeply, even the coolest and most candid discussion is unlikely to change attitudes very much or very soon.

None of this is intended to show that the suggested approaches to these problems are unworkable or should be rejected but rather two things: (i) candor, patience, tact and ability to think and talk clearly about morals are required of people who, however liberal their own attitudes toward sexual relations, still take seriously and want to minimize the undesirable consequences that can result when other people have conflicting views, attitudes and expectations; and (ii) while fortune may favor some people in some of their sexual involvements, it is not realistic to hope that in every case there will be a solution in which one can both make love joyously with a person one cares for and not be concerned about the undesirable consequences we have been contemplating. Anyone who cares about those consequences must sometimes abandon hope of a sexual consummation, or that consummation must await an adjustment of attitudes and convictions. Sometimes the attempt to reach understanding, whether with a sex partner or with other concerned persons, will have just the opposite effect. In short, sexual involvements can be quite difficult for a person who tries to live in such a way as to avoid deception and sorry human relationships. One may for that reason disavow concern for these things, but only at the price of being unable to regard oneself as a responsible human being.

Similar questions arise quite frequently in marriage. Here the interesting case is one in which a marriage is as happy as one could wish, and so there is no desire either to end it or to compensate for its tedium with other pleasures, but one of the partners becomes romantically interested in someone else. Few people are so devoted to a spouse as to lose all sexual interest in other persons, and it can often appear that it should be quite possible to have the joy of a love affair without any adverse effect on a happy marriage. Some couples have an explicit agreement that either of them is entirely free to go ahead in such a case, but such agreements often have the intellectual but not the emotional assent of the parties. Hence whether or not there is such an agreement, there is likely to be the problem that a spouse would be deeply pained on learning of such an affair.

To avoid the verbal contrivances involved in writing about this without reference to gender, let us suppose that it is a woman who is contemplating an affair, and she reflects that although her husband would in all likelihood be very wounded by it, he really has no reason to be hurt. Her pleasure in this other man does not reflect any change in her feeling for him; and it would be quite possible, if only he could understand this, for their good relationship to continue as happily as before. He may also be concerned about other things, for example, about the embarrassment he may suffer if friends and acquaintances learn of the affair; but here again, she may reflect, it is old-fashioned and unnecessary to be embarrassed, and if only he could acquire some independence of mind, he could shrug off anxieties as to what friends may think. The important thing, she thinks, is whether she does lack respect for him, not whether his friends think she does; and he must know, from the quality of their life together, what she really feels.

Here again we have a case in which it is attitudes that are thought to be unwise or unnecessary which give rise to a moral problem, and a question whether, because they are unwise, they and their consequences can be ignored. Those consequences can be avoided if the wife can have her affair and keep it secret; and the deception she thereby practices can be given a justification on the grounds that, although it would be painful to her husband to know of the affair, it ought not to trouble him, or so she believes. Yet deception, even when so justified, is something that one would morally prefer not to practice. It is also quite dangerous, because affairs are hard to keep secret for very long, and the deception is likely to add to the husband's pain, should he find out.

If one therefore deems it best to be open, one can hardly seek a spouse's permission to embark on a specific love affair. It is too much to ask. There is a large difference between reaching an understanding in principle, when no specific entanglements are contemplated, and asking a spouse, "Do you mind if I make love with so and so?" However, it is possible to be open in a different way: to go ahead without consent, but tell a spouse what is happening, say how wonderful it is, say that one is not asking permission to continue it, but declare an intention to prove, as time passes, that there is no cause to grieve or be hurt.

Two things about such a line of action are fairly clear: first, that it might work in some cases, and that if it did, there might remain little that was morally unsatisfactory. What would remain is chiefly: (i) that a vow of fidelity had been broken, if such a vow had been taken, and (ii) that a course of action had been pursued which, although ultimately successful, was originally very unlikely to succeed. If the risks are grave, and the chance of avoiding them slight, it can be irresponsible to have done something even if in fact things turned out well. Secondly, in an average case, the bold line of action described does stand a poor chance of success; and if what had been a good marriage breaks up, or becomes an unhappy one, what is lost will normally be much greater than what is gained.

There is a natural tendency, in reading a discussion such as the foregoing, to keep waiting for a conclusion to be drawn: to want to know what a person faced with this problem should do, or to wonder if the conclusion will be that extramarital love affairs are always wrong, or that they are wrong when managed in this way, but not when done that way, and so on.

What I want to suggest by contrast is that *all* of what has been said is the conclusion. We are not here trying to make a moral decision, but to illustrate the variety of considerations that will bear on a decision in different cases. Moreover, there is no perfectly ideal thing to do about most real life problems, but whatever course of action we settle on is liable to have its regrettable aspects. Hence what we need generally is not a verdict — right or wrong — but an appreciation of the various aspects of a proposed line of action, such as may help us to choose between it and other alternatives.

In this first part of Chapter 2, we have brought out some of the main ways in which there can be moral problems about the conduct of our sex lives. In doing this we have largely ignored the claims of what was called the "monogamous principle." Our question has been: *if* making love is not immoral *just* because the persons involved are not man and wife, what other moral restrictions may there be on our sex lives?

Roughly and broadly, the answer suggested was that we can go wrong: (a) when there is a risk of an unwanted pregnancy, and (b) when there are any of the various risks of deception, grief and hard feeling, or moral confusion that arise from the moral and other attitudes that, for good or ill, surround sex in our culture.

Our discussion of these matters may have contained little that is not fairly obvious once it is spelled out. If anything new has been achieved, it is mostly in the spelling out of what can be strangely difficult to see clearly. Being ourselves personally involved in the business, with all the fancies and tensions that come with that involvement, perhaps we have difficulty standing back and critically observing the scene that includes ourselves. We are like people in a maze which, however simple it may be, can be surveyed from within only with the greatest difficulty.

Our emphasis on the possibilities of moral fault may have generated the impression that sexual behavior is haunted in every case and on all sides by moral problems; and it is important to see that this is not true. Apart from claims stemming from the monogamous principle, given only rudimentary candor and concern for other people's interests, and some good fortune in one's sexual friendships, it is not only possible to lead a vigorous sex life without moral fault, but in today's world it happens very frequently. And if more of us were more clearheaded about these matters, it might be even more common.

WHAT IS GOOD ABOUT MONOGAMY?

We have not so far addressed ourselves in any way to the question of the merits of the monogamous principle; and were we to agree with its defenders that any sexual activity outside of marriage is immoral, the conclusions we have reached so far might only show in which cases sinners can be doubly sinful.

The aim of this section, therefore, will be to carry out some evaluation of what we have been calling "the monogamous principle."

We might begin by making a distinction between two theses: on the one hand, the strong claim that lifelong marriage is the only arrangement on which a man and a woman can properly make love, and on the other, the claim that the institution of marriage is a very good thing and eminently worth preserving, and that anything that interferes with its preservation is morally regrettable, and how regrettable it is depends on how greatly it threatens the institution.

During the present time of moral upheaval, it tends to be the former thesis that looms large in our thinking, and is upheld or rejected; and this is unfortunate, if it excludes from consideration more moderate views, such as the latter.

The strong thesis, perhaps because it is difficult to defend, is not often backed by any arguments, but is put across as a point of morals so utterly fundamental as to be one of the bases of a moral outlook. When anything is treated as fundamental, one can appeal to it as a reason for favoring or opposing other things, but to defend it in any way is to deny its status as a basic tenet.

The tendency to treat the monogamous principle as fundamental in this way has some unfortunate consequences. In the first place it presents the moral question about the institution of marriage as one about which it is impossible to deliberate. It generates an atmosphere in which the monogamous principle must simply either be accepted or rejected, and in which to reject it is to act immorally. It thus converts moral disagreement from being an effort of concerned people to work out what is best, to being a struggle between angels and devils, a struggle in which, argument being ruled out, there remain mostly less attractive and respectful methods.

Secondly and somewhat paradoxically, treating the monogamous principle as morally basic tends quite strongly to weaken the institution of marriage. By presenting marriage as something that simply must be accepted, on the one hand it comes across in many people's eyes as a requirement to be resented, while on the other it precludes more than desultory efforts to depict marriage as desirable, and thereby increase the number of people who enter it eagerly, work at preserving it and are not easily discouraged if it proves difficult.

To make this last point as clear as possible, we need to recognize a distinction between thinking marriage a good thing, and wanting to live with a certain person, and so accepting marriage as the condition on which that is possible. Many people, without particularly regarding marriage itself as a good thing, are still eager for it as a way of living with someone they love. It is when they could live with this person without marrying, and without such practical disadvantages as social disapproval, and yet choose to enter marriage, that they show some interest in marriage itself.

It is not easy to construct a justification of the strong monogamous principle, at least not one sufficient to show that it would be wrong to arrange things in any other way. One might imagine a community in which everyone would enter marriage only as virgins, be faithful to one another in the face of every temptation, and stay together as long as they live. If we visited a community in which this was cheerfully done and any other way of arranging these things was considered unthinkable, we might admire and stand in awe of those people; but the fact that it is splendid does not in the least show that any different arrangement would be morally wrong. It might be reprehensible if I were to join this community and then proceed to violate all its conventions, but it would be wrong, not because of the moral necessity of the conventions, but because thwarting them would create so much disruption and grief.

It is therefore not sufficient to argue that the monogamous principle is always good simply because its violation causes pain and social dislocation. There are many ways in which marriage can be a good thing, and there is much to be said in favor of family life as a way of caring for and nurturing children. There are also ways in which liberal sex practices can spoil marriages and either break up families or lower the quality of family life. Hence something good can often be adversely affected by departures from the monogamous principle. However, the fact that marriage and family life can be good does not at all show that they are the only or even the best ways of arranging these matters; nor does the fact that liberal sex practices can adversely affect these often good things show that departures from the monogamous principle are wrong *whenever* they occur. The most it shows is that when a marriage is in fact a good one, and when a love affair would in fact adversely affect it, such departures are wrong. If a good marriage is not adversely affected, or if a poor one is, then at least on the reasoning we are now considering, nothing is morally amiss.

Moreover, there is a suspicion of circularity at work here, inasmuch as at least very often it is acceptance of the monogamous principle by one of the marriage partners that is the source of the intense dismay if the other has a love affair, and thus of the adverse effect. Persons who are not strongly imbued with the ideal of sexual fidelity will either not be offended or not be so intensely offended if their spouse has a love affair.

Here is one of the junctures where the hard question arises whether, if something unfortunate is likely to happen in a large number of cases as a result of a certain form of behavior, it is sound policy to represent that behavior as wrong whenever it occurs, in spite of the fact that it can often occur without those consequences ensuing. Many people, even without being morally indignant, are very wounded by a spouse's infidelity, and many marriages founder or go sour on that account; however, there are also people who are untroubled by it. Is it best to represent the infidelity as categorically wrong, on the grounds that otherwise too many people will falsely suppose theirs to be a case in which the undesirable consequence will not ensue?

If we do this, there is misrepresentation, and thus immorality, albeit of a mild form, built right into our official ethics. It may be, however, that sometimes there is no responsible way of avoiding this. It perhaps depends in part on how much effort a community is willing to put into moral education. If, instead of providing people with an all-purpose set of dos and don'ts to follow, we were prepared to spend long hours teaching people to make responsible individualized moral decisions without fakery or self-deception, there might be little need ever to represent anything as categorically wrong just because in a great many cases there would be undesirable consequences. Our unwillingness to expend that much effort on moral education is one source of moral confusion, because inevitably some people perceive the falsity that otherwise we can hardly avoid building into our official ethics.

For the purpose of our deliberations, however, it may not be necessary to have any view as to what would be sound official ethics. We are unlikely to be able to change that very much, and what we are trying to decide is how one might responsibly arrange one's life *whatever* the official ethic holds, or other people may think. We have seen that the convictions of other people often figure as one of the important facts to be reckoned with, but there is a difference between reckoning with these convictions and accepting them. Indeed if one accepts them they will no longer be something to be reckoned with, because there will be no question of acting contrary to them.

So far, we have failed to find any remotely adequate justification of the strong form of the monogamous principle. This failure does not itself show that no justification is possible, but it may be significant that a principle so old and so much insisted on should require so much effort to justify.

It was suggested that if the monogamous principle is presented as a basic moral tenet, there will be something incoherent about arguing for it, and that if it is therefore insisted on rather than recommended, it will on the one hand come across as a requirement arbitrarily imposed, while on the other fewer people will regard marriage as itself a good thing, as distinct from wanting to live with a certain person and accepting marriage as a condition by which cohabitation is permissible.

Since there are considerable disadvantages to the strong thesis, it is at least initially much more promising to try the weaker view: that marriage is for various reasons a very good thing, and that anything that interferes with its preservation is morally regrettable, and regrettable in proportion as it threatens the institution.

That is the claim that will be evaluated in the following two subsections. It will be important to be clear as to some of the differences between it and the strong thesis.

1. Since marriage is praised or recommended, rather than insisted on, it will not necessarily be the only desirable form of relationship between a man and a woman, but will be an arrangement they may choose if they are impressed by what can be said in its favor.

2. While it will be possible to claim that the marriage institution can be preserved only if it is the only available arrangement, that claim becomes testable, and may or may not test out successfully.

3. Whereas given the strong thesis, the surrounding prohibitions against premarital and extramarital sex would be (and have been) treated as basic moral tenets and therefore as not requiring a defence, the prohibitions would now hold only if, or to the extent that, or in the cases where, they threatened the institution of marriage.

4. Whereas given the strong thesis, there is at least room for a concept of "marriage proper" as a union of two people who are virgins prior to marriage and who avoid extramarital love affairs, on the weaker thesis there is either no concept of marriage proper, or it means something like "a successful union of two people."

In the ensuing discussion there will sometimes be a possible confusion between two questions: whether a certain practice threatens the institution of marriage—that is, the tendency of the community generally to respect it, want it, care about it—and the question whether a given marriage will be threatened by a particular course of action; for example, whether Stephen and Mary's marriage will be threatened if Stephen has a love affair.

Questions of the former kind are very often raised in discussions of these matters, but they do not often help much, because they are uncommonly difficult to know how to answer. The institution of marriage has remained remarkably vigorous over the centuries in spite of the fact that there has always been a great deal of premarital and extramarital sexual activity, and there have also been many marriages that for other reasons count as very bad advertisements for the institution. If marriage has survived all these assaults, it is not easy to suggest what actions of ours will put it in jeopardy.

Moreover, it is not very clear what would show that the institution of marriage had suffered a setback. If, some years after some change of attitude had become widespread, we found that many fewer people married, but that a very much larger proportion of those who did did so freely and eagerly, thinking it was an excellent arrangement, would we conclude that the institution had suffered or benefited?

Again, our calculation or hunches as to the probable effect on the institution of some social change are likely to be based on the way we find things often work out now, when the change in question has not yet occurred, or occurred widely. For example, if at the time at which we are making our calculations the moral climate makes it very awkward socially for two people who live together without marrying, many people will marry for no better reason than to avoid this social awkwardness, and the immediate effect of a relaxation of the disapproval of such behavior will likely be that fewer people marry. We have no way of calculating, however, what the long-term effect will be, because we do not know what disadvantages of cohabitation, through widespread experience of it, may come to be part of the popular wisdom, and we do not know whether, when there is more choice as to whether to marry, the charms of marriage will come to be more effectively advertised.

For these various reasons, questions as to the effect of this or that on the institution of marriage will be largely avoided as being imponderable. Much more manageable, at least in many cases, are such questions as what Mary will do if Stephen has an affair. Of course we are not going to answer any such questions, because our examples are hypothetical; but the fact that some Stephens could answer them with some assurance of being right will often be significant.

What Are the Moral Alternatives to Marriage?

In the first part of this chapter, one of the conclusions suggested was that, by the criteria we are using, while there were various cases in which making love was quite clearly morally objectionable, it was by no means always so. In those deliberations, however, we specifically excluded the question whether sexual activity might be wrong whenever it was not between man and wife. That is to say, we allowed that our conclusions might be nullified if we had to accept some of the moral claims entailed by the monogamous principle.

In the introduction to our discussion of the monogamous principle, it was suggested in the first place that the monogamous principle is often presented as being so basic morally that to sing its praises would be to weaken the moral claim it made. If we sing its praises we will be treating it, depending on how highly it can be praised, as a fairly or an extremely good thing, but not as something so fundamental that any alternative to or departure from it would be wrong, unless by departing from it one makes it seriously less likely that oneself or other people will participate in this good thing, and more likely that less desirable alternatives will prevail.

It was proposed, secondly, not to accept the idea that the monogamous principle was "one of the basics," but rather to inquire what can be said on its behalf; and it was recognized that in doing this we would be placing it on a very different footing, in which, while its claims might turn out to be less stringent than heretofore, there might be the advantage that more people could be persuaded of its charms, and want it as a good thing, rather than accepting it as a moral necessity.

Thirdly, it was suggested that, whereas presenting the monogamous principle as morally basic made it unimportant whether, for example, by having a premarital sex life one became less likely to marry or to be a good spouse, since on that view premarital sex is wrong whatever the result, if we examine the monogamous principle under the second thesis, premarital sex is wrong if (a) marriage is not only an excellent thing, but much better than available alternatives, and (b) premarital sex either makes the occurrence of this excellent thing less likely, or makes it likely to be less excellent.

Finally, it was argued that while questions as to the effect on marriage of various forms of sexual activity can be answered with some confidence on an individual basis, it is unlikely that we can predict the effects of various forms of behavior on the *institution* of marriage—or not with enough confidence to enable us to base any moral conclusions on such predictions.

In all of this we have been working out a form for our inquiry to take, and have not as yet posed any questions as to the actual merits of marriage and family life. Such questions will be the business of the present subsection, and the two following.

We might begin by reiterating the important distinction between thinking it a good thing to unite oneself on a permanent basis with another person, and wanting to marry a particular person. Catherine may want very much to marry David, without having any particular opinion as to whether it is a good thing to unite oneself with another person on a permanent basis. If she both thinks marriage a good thing and wants to marry David, there will be more contributing to the success of the union than if she either has no view as to the merits of uniting with him on a permanent basis, or accepts it reluctantly as the lesser of two evils.

Probably fewer people nowadays have a strong conviction of the desirability of the married state itself; and we could usefully ask why not, and whether there are nevertheless good reasons for valuing marriage.

An obvious partial explanation for the faintness of the current passion for marriage is the fact that the official reason for its importance has all along been that it is a state appointed by God, and that to "put a marriage asunder" is to undo something God has done. God is, it is true, represented as having had reasons for so appointing, but these are seldom mentioned when marriage is defended, presumably because if God favors something, that is all we need to know. Today religion exerts less of an influence, and those who are religious are less inclined to accept as the will of God everything the established church chooses so to designate. Moreover the reasons assigned for God's preference in this matter —namely, the begetting of children, their upbringing "in the fear and nurture of the Lord", "the avoidance of fornication" and the mutual society, comfort and help of two people — are ends that might well be achieved in other ways. God's alleged preference therefore seems, just on the basis of the assigned reasons, somewhat arbitrary.

Secondly, one of the important purposes of marriage, the long-term protection of the woman, is no longer as necessary as it once was. At a time when there were very few ways in which a woman could earn her own living and be independent, it was extremely important that, having spent her years of greatest attractiveness married to a man, she should not then be abandoned and left to eke out a meagre existence as a housekeeper, lady's companion or seamstress. But now, when there are more and better jobs available for women, and a climate in which a woman who prefers independence is not regarded as a freak or a failure, economic security is no longer such a compelling reason, and would become even less compelling if marriage came to be regarded as normally a temporary arrangement, or at any event normally an arrangement not interfering with a woman's having a career. The old concept of marriage created its own justification: it cast women in a role that made it vitally necessary for them to have the protection that only marriage could provide.

In this it somewhat resembles one of God's alleged reasons for instituting marriage: to save us from fornication, that is, from making love outside of marriage. If there were no such institution as marriage, there could be no such thing as fornication, and nothing from which marriage could save us. When marriage and hence fornication both exist, it is possible to marry to avoid fornication; but it is no more possible to institute marriage as a way of avoiding fornication than it is to institute parking rules as a way of avoiding their violation. One can introduce parking rules as a way of avoiding parking chaos; but there can be no parking violations before the introduction of any rules, and similarly no fornication before the institution of marriage.

Yet it is possible for something that has been created for one set of reasons, whether good or bad, to prove valuable in unexpected ways, and marriage has been found valuable, by great numbers of people, in ways over and above the obvious ones of providing companionship, security, and a way of bringing up children.

Many people find it unsatisfying, over the long term, to live just for themselves. There are some occupations in which, to varying degrees, one can regard oneself as living for others—the practice of medicine perhaps, or social work — but most people divide their lives into two parts, their vocation and the life they lead after working hours, and many find the latter unsatisfying if it is largely taken up with pleasing themselves. There are other ways of relieving this dissatisfaction, working for charitable organizations or political parties, for example, but marriage is a most comprehensive way. It is not an occasional commitment, but occupies all one's time and resources; it does not have to be pursued—one does not have to keep looking for things to do, ways to be useful—but takes over and provides endless outlets for energy and creativity; and its rewards come, not in the form of gratitude or praise (for which most people have a limited appetite), or of self-congratulation, but in enjoying the pleasure and wellbeing of people one cares about.

Even in a society where divorce is available, the ideal of the permanence of marriage can have consequences that appeal quite strongly to some people. No matter how delightful two people find one another, both in the short run and in the long run it can be quite difficult for them to live together. They can prove to have very different attitudes to the fine details of joint living: to the management of money, the arrangement of mealtimes, the choice of furniture, the entertaining of friends, how to spend a Saturday afternoon, the roles of husband and wife with regard to shopping, cooking, housecleaning. Such differences can, of course, be resolved by mutual and often grudging submission and self-sacrifice, but they can also be handled more inventively, by coming up with new alternatives, and by teaching each other to see the charms and possibilities of another style and pattern of life. In this way, year after year, the ideal of the permanence of marriage can enhance our lives by encouraging us to devise creative solutions to a thousand problems.

For such reasons as these, it is possible to want marriage independently of one's desire to marry a certain person; and year in year out through the course of a marriage, the former desire can contribute immensely to its success.

In trying to ascertain what is good about marriage, it is probably a mistake to cite examples of wonderful marriages, describing their various joys and benefits. In the first place, while we all know of such marriages (and if we do not, we are not likely to be much interested in assurances that they do sometimes occur), we know too of marriages that are full of hostility and woe. In the second place it will rarely be clear how much of the excellence of a good marriage is due to the fact that it is a marriage, and not some other arrangement. Who can say whether things would have been different if George and Marjorie, whose marriage has been very rewarding, had lived together rather than marrying—especially if the cultural climate did not itself penalize them for not marrying?

We need to concentrate just on the benefits that flow from the fact that the arrangement is conceived to be either permanent or difficult to dissolve. The chief value of that fact is that, by putting out of mind the question of dissolving the arrangement when difficulties arise, it is likely to make couples approach the myriad problems of joint living with much more intelligence, flexibility and forbearance than they otherwise might; and since even the most enthusiastic couples are likely to experience painful difficulties in the course of living together over any length of time, this is an extremely important consideration.

It is not clear, however, that either permanence or any of the other familiar joys and benefits of marriage make it such an incomparably fine arrangement as to be the only one a community should offer people who want to live together. For one thing, the ambition to pursue marriage inventively, and with flexibility and patience, is by no means universal among married people; and even those who have it do not always pursue it with all the skill the task can require.

For another, if one had a choice of conjugal arrangements, one of which was marriage, there is something logically unsatisfactory about the idea of choosing marriage for the reason that its permanence would provide a motivation for seeing to it that it worked: if one already had the ambition to be resourceful in the pursuit of a conjugal arrangement, it is not clear that one would need the added impetus that the official permanence of the arrangement might provide. It is true that people might, for fear of faltering in their resolve, fix things so that they had better not falter, but it would be extra cautious of them to do so, and only in a small percentage of cases would this added assurance be necessary.

Hence the reasoning here, while it provides weak support at best, works better for policy makers than for individuals. Policy makers might decide to make marriage the only available conjugal arrangement because then more people would form unions soberly and advisedly than if there were various arrangements amongst which they could choose; but individuals cannot very well esteem marriage for that reason without already recognizing the importance of sobriety and advisedness.

How Binding Are Marriage Vows?

In the Church of England's *Book of Common Prayer*, the form for the solemnization of matrimony provides that the priest shall say to the intending husband: "Wilt thou love her, comfort her, honor and keep her, in sickness and in health; and, forsaking all others, keep thee only unto her, so long as ye both shall live?" It further provides that "the man shall answer, I will." There is a similar undertaking prescribed for the intending wife, who, however, does not promise to comfort, and does promise to obey and serve.

Other marriage ceremonies, whether religious or civil, differ in some particulars from this, but whenever there is one law concerning such matters as divorce or the property rights of marriage partners, what counts as being married cannot differ very widely from case to case; and so we can discuss the Church of England's form as being at least quite typical of what is promised in marriage, and the differences between one ceremony and another will not be found to make much difference to our discussion.

Some of the things promised here are clearer than others. It could be quite difficult to decide, in many actual cases, whether one had failed to honor one's spouse, and since "keeping" is promised by both parties, and therefore can hardly mean support financially, it is a matter for speculation what it does include.

Also, while honoring, keeping, comforting, obeying and serving, whatever exactly they consist in, are all actions that can be performed at will and can therefore be promised, it is not clear that loving is an action, and therefore not clear that it can be promised. I can be asked to help Martha, and thereupon do it, but I cannot be asked to love her and thereupon do it. I either love her or I do not; and while there are some things I can do that may contribute to making me love her, or to preserving my love for her, I have no control over whether they work or not.

However, some officially prescribed promises are clearer than others in these regards, so let us assume that there is a moderately clear set of promises, whatever they may be, and ask what follows morally from the fact that one has so promised? Many people, without regarding themselves as being morally remiss, are inclined to treat marriage vows as being of no significance, and to think that whether it is wrong to break them is a question of whether it would be unfair or excessively damaging to one of the parties, or of what would be best in the long run for both parties or for others affected, particularly children, or of whether or how ungrudgingly one spouse consents to a departure from what was promised.

The prevalence of this attitude seems quite paradoxical in view of the fact that the same people are not nearly so inclined to say of other promises — about meeting people, doing things for them, paying money — that the promise itself is of no significance, while the marriage vows are far more momentous and more solemn than any of these. Yet it may be their very momentousness and solemnity that makes these vows less binding.

In the first place, it is plausible to maintain that a promise is binding only to the extent that its performance is reasonably within the power of the person promising. If I promise to return your book by Thursday or to go with you to Montreal, then while it may prove unexpectedly difficult for me to do these things, generally I can overcome the difficulties, and you have some right to complain of bad faith if I fail; but if I promise to enjoy a certain film, to become a millionaire, or to be your friend for twenty years, then no matter how serious you take me to be, you would not have a clear right to complain if I failed to deliver. Now, a marriage vow can be seen as a promise of the latter kind. It makes undertakings with regard to a very long stretch of time, in the course of which a couple may become entirely different persons, with ambitions, tastes, idiosyncrasies or emotional attachments or aversions that could not initially be foreseen, and given which it would be utterly absurd for them to marry. That being the case, it seems reasonable to treat such vows at a minimum as implicitly containing some such clause as "assuming you are substantially the person I believe you to be, and that neither of us changes, as the years go by, in ways more extreme than are common to human beings as they grow older."

Secondly, the conditions under which people make marriage vows are significantly different from those under which they make other promises. Whereas it is standard elsewhere for a person promising freely to choose what will be undertaken, there is no choice, at least as to the minimum form of a marriage vow. If a couple promised to love, honor and cherish for a specified length of time, say three years, they would not be deemed to be married; nor would they, if they so promised "for as long as it shall be mutually agreeable." If John and Mary fall in love and decide to get married, they do not necessarily want to swear lifelong fidelity, or want not to either. They perhaps want only to live together with legal approval, and have a house and children, but on the wedding day they find the words of a promise put into their mouths. The *occasion* is made solemn by the ancient ritual and the music; but they do not solemnly promise. They simply say whatever they are told to say and do whatever one has to do to be married in our culture.

It would be different if, when the marriage was being considered, Mary had said: "John, I will marry you, but only if you will solemnly promise to be faithful to me for the rest of our lives," and he had agreed; or again it would be different if in the community there was a choice of standard conjugal arrangements, each with its own name and with different rights and obligations, and a couple could decide, for example, whether to marry, sub-marry or super-marry. It would then be clear that in deciding, say, to super-marry, a couple were specifically committing themselves to that set of obligations and rights.

As things are, however, although it is sometimes possible on request to make minor changes in the wording of the marriage vows, a magistrate or a priest does not routinely present a couple with a choice, and hence it is reasonable to take the position that marriage vows have no more meaning than is either attached to them by those who make them, or attributed to them from time to time by the community.

If attitudes changed in such a way that most people were

altogether complacent about the dissolution of marriages, at least when cheerfully arranged, or about sexual infidelity, but the standard marriage ceremony still included promises of permanence and fidelity, no one could take the marriage vows literally. The ceremony would be regarded perhaps as a nice old tradition, but if it committed people to anything, it would be only to what the community then required morally of people who married: perhaps such things as that they should not casually or offhandedly dissolve the union, that they should not do so to the undue detriment of either partner or on account of such misfortunes as illness or financial setbacks.

Although the preceding paragraph was presented hypothetically, something not altogether unlike the situation it describes presently prevails. Few of us take the marriage vows literally; the ceremony is indulgently regarded as a nice old tradition; and what is expected of people who marry is not much more than a general standard of honesty, fairness and concern for each other's welfare. (That standard of course can be quite a lot, but what is omitted is any or much expectation that people will adhere to it *just* because they promised.)

The fact that divorce is permissible is concrete proof that we do not take the marriage vows entirely literally. Wherever the same people who formulate the official vows also either make divorce possible or favor divorce under some conditions, the net import of a clause such as "as long as you both shall live" can only be taken to be "as long as you remain legally married" (or, if a church favors divorce, but not under all the conditions in which it is legally possible, "as long as conditions do not prevail in which we approve of divorce").

One does not have to *want* marriage vows to be somewhat empty words, in order to see that they must be so regarded; indeed, it seems deplorable, and a kind of rot that is liable to spread to other areas of life, if the words we say about such an important matter, however unclear some of them may be, cannot be taken to commit us to whatever they clearly *do* mean.

This is not a state of affairs without a remedy. Among the possible remedies might be:

1. Rewriting the marriage vows in such a way that they: (a) are clearer and do not contain words that could mean anything or nothing, as it was suggested that "love," "honor," and "keep" in the Church of England form could; and (b) express the essentials of what is in fact seriously expected of married people, so that there would not, for example, be the discrepancy between the vow and the possibility of divorce.

2. If the conditions above seemed to require too liberal a standard form, or to preclude people from undertaking a very demanding form of marriage if they wished, two or more standard forms could be worked out; and it could be provided, for example, that divorce would not be so available to anyone who had opted for the most demanding form. This would partially relieve the difficulty we found in the fact that people intending marriage have little choice in what they undertake.

3. A remedy for the fact that it is unreasonable to hold a person to a promise going beyond what is in his practical control might lie in including some such form of words as "will endeavor with all my heart" in such parts of any vows as have that feature.

Do Liberal Sexual Attitudes Threaten the Family?

Questions about the value of the family as an institution arise in connection with sexual conduct if, or to the extent that, a relaxed or open attitude towards sexual liaisons tends to make the family unstable. If there is that tendency then the question arises whether the institution of the family is such a valuable thing that anything that threatens it is therefore wrong and to be avoided.

Whether open or liberal sexual attitudes are indeed a threat to the family is a question of fact that we cannot attempt to settle. Is a person who has tangled sexually with a number of people less likely to marry, or less likely upon marrying to take seriously the responsibilities of parenthood or the difficult business of adjusting to year-round, day-in day-out union with another person? Is such a person more likely to have extramarital affairs, and are such affairs necessarily detrimental to a marriage? In considering these questions, one must distinguish between what it seems reasonable to expect and what actually occurs in practice. Also, one must realize that existing information as to the practical results of various forms of sexual behavior is likely to be unreliable for at least two reasons.

The first is that such information will generally have been gathered from a moral climate in which strong feelings of disapproval of liberal sex practices are common, and these feelings will affect the outcome. If sexual attitudes were to become more liberal over a period of, say, twenty years, the effects on marriage of the gradual liberalization would be different at the beginning of the twenty-year period from what they would be at the end.

Secondly, many other factors will make a difference, one of them being whether we drift rather aimlessly into the new moral climate, or go into it deliberately and intentionally. In the latter event, we might teach people new attitudes, and thereby considerably reduce the amount of anguish and confusion that usually prevail in times of social change.

If we had some statistics on what percentage of marriages either failed or deteriorated owing to the love affairs of one or other of the partners, they would show nothing unless they were drawn from a community where not only had liberal attitudes prevailed long enough for most people to come to share them, but also, owing to some teaching efforts, the liberal attitudes were largely held in a positive way, as part of people's conception of civilized living. Since we are contemplating a considerable departure from anything that now exists, statistics with such a base are unlikely to be available, and we must make do with enlightened guesses.

When we thus set about our guessing, there are considerations that reasonably support conflicting expectations. For example, one might argue that a person with a good deal of sexual experience is likely to have acquired a deeper than usual understanding of other people, and hence to make a more mature choice of marriage partner. On the other hand, it might be said that people who make intimate alliances somewhat casually may often have too casual an attitude to marriage — although again some of the people who do not see themselves as morally bound to marry will, if they so choose, take it particularly seriously.

While devoutly believing in the monogamous principle is likely to make a person particularly determined to make a marriage succeed, a person who, because of that belief, has made love with only one person is likely to be especially curious as to how it might be with someone else, resentful of the belief that frustrated this curiosity, and thus led to experiment.

People whose principles allowed for sexual intimacy as fortune dictated might not be much grieved if fortune dictated such a relationship between a marriage partner and some third person, so that the marriages of such people might more often survive casual love affairs. On the other hand, anyone who attached the kind of almost religious importance to marriage that goes with a monogamous conviction, even if aggrieved by a marriage partner's wanderings, would have a particularly strong stimulus to forgiveness and reconciliation, while the same conviction would in other cases make its holder entirely unable to accept a spouse's love affair. Moreover, forgiveness is not often wholehearted, and when it is not, its overtones of moral superiority may have a ruinous effect.

Thus on the whole, what one might expect is that the effect on marriage of liberal sexual attitudes, at least at the point at which such attitudes had become widespread, would be very mixed — sometimes beneficial and sometimes detrimental — but probably not more mixed or more detrimental than the effect of a common conviction that sex should be confined only to one's marriage partner, coupled with the thwarting of that conviction which, as long as sex remains the powerful drive it is, will be a feature of the lives of a great many people.

Suppose, however, that this speculation is wrong, and that the institution of marriage *is* seriously threatened by any liberalization of attitudes towards sexual alliances: would that be a strong argument against such liberalization? Are marriage and family life such uncommonly good things that it is unthinkable to permit any practice that adversely affects them? Or are they, although not unmixed blessings, at least the only workable arrangements for solving some of life's basic and perennial problems?

There is no contesting that we need some way of providing children with love, care, education, security and happiness; and while other systems for doing so are quite imaginable, the family is not only the only large-scale provision we now make for this purpose (orphanages and foster homes aside), but is generally a method well suited to the purpose. There are many and sad exceptions, but generally in the family a child receives concentrated and individual attention. Even unattractive children are loved and cared for by their parents in a way and to a degree that would be unlikely in persons hired for the purpose. Because of differences in the convictions, tastes, activities, sorrows and journeys of different families, children acquire an individuality in the family that would be less common or less marked if we grew up in most other ways one can think of. Above all, there is a warmth, solidarity and security about the small family group that is important, not only because it is agreeable in itself, but for its effects on the growth of personality.

Parents too can find family life deeply rewarding, however exhausting and demanding it may be. To join with someone you love in the creation of a manner of life that jointly satisfies your tastes and interests, to follow with affection and anxiety the growth and development of children, to have something beyond oneself for which to strive and on which to count are experiences that very large numbers of people find excellent.

There are, of course, darker sides to this rosy picture. Marriages range all the way from being joyful and altogether satisfying, through being a bit tiresome but tolerable enough, to being nightmarish. Some parents with the best will in the world do a dreadful job of bringing up their children; and the children of parents whose marriage is nightmarish may grow up in an atmosphere of violence, hostility and insecurity that not only sours an important part of their lives, but can have a harmful effect on their personalities.

In evaluating marriage as an institution, given that there are good things and bad things about it, there are at least three important questions about the bad things: (i) how widespread and acute are they? (ii) how do they compare in extent and gravity with the probable imperfections of alternative systems that might be contrived to meet the same needs? and (iii) how endemic are they: are there ways in which they could be reduced or eliminated?

It is common knowledge that some marriages are indescribably awful, and that many are joyless and dull. It is not clear what we would do with more exact information than this. If we knew that only thirty-seven percent of marriages were rewarding enough that the partners would, if they had it to do over, make the same choice of mate, but perhaps also knew that in seventy-two percent of marriages, children were reared in a manner at least acceptable, and the parents did at least provide one another with help and companionship, even if there were little or no mutual enjoyment, it is not clear that we would be in a better position to decide as to the merits of the institution.

It might be, however, that if, as well as knowing such things, we also had reason to think that marriage, although it was not so very often an excellent thing, was more often excellent and less often atrocious, and in the great mass of in-between cases was at least as good as the workable alternatives, we would have sufficient reason to push for its preservation. Even so, we would not have a reason to fix it as the *only* acceptable arrangement.

We are not, however, in a good position to compare it with "workable alternatives." For one thing, we do not know what all of these might be; and for another, those that have been tried will very often have been tried under adverse conditions. When something is tried in the face of social disapproval, it may work out badly or fail just because of that disapproval; and similarly if some of the participants in an experiment are social rebels, and enter it more than anything as a form of rebellion, they may not apply themselves to the tasks and problems of the project with all the requisite good will and inventiveness, and hence it may fail.

The significant test could only occur when some alternative arrangement was tried under all the social conditions that have contributed to making marriage at least successful enough to survive over a long stretch of time; for example, people being prepared for it from an early age, the laws and customs of the community being such as not to make it a disadvantageous arrangement, it being generally depicted as a good thing and worthy of felicitation when it occurs. Alternative arrangements that we may contemplate will often not have been tried at all, and if they have been tried, it will of course not be under such conditions as these, and therefore evidence as to their success will generally be of very limited value.

It is an engaging idea that a group of congenial people should join together and cope co-operatively with the day-to-day chores and problems of living. If there are children, they would be looked after by those members of the group who most enjoy children; the cooking, shopping and housekeeping would be done either by those who like it, or on a rotation system; and the funds for the material support of the group would come from some members of the group taking outside employment. In this way, each member of the group could largely avoid what is found tiresome and concentrate on what is agreeable, and each person, by specializing in some one or some few activities, could learn to perform those activities better than if everyone's activities were spread out over a broader range, with a resulting improvement in the quality of cooking, child care, and other skills.

In practice, however, there are problems. It is hard enough to find one person with whom one can live happily, without having to find six or ten. If one does find a congenial group, it will not necessarily or even very likely be the case that any or enough of them enjoy caring for children or cooking or any of the other regular chores. If tasks are assigned on a rotation system, it will time and again prove inconvenient to perform one's assigned task, and there will be constant negotiations and resentments when the system breaks down. Some members will perform their duties conscientiously and well, but others will be remiss or incompetent, and their shortcomings will be resented. If some members are lax about their contributions to the communal welfare, others who would otherwise not be will cut back their efforts so as not to do more than their fair share, with the result that the standards of cooking, cleanliness and so on will fall. If some of the members who go out to work earn very much more than others, they may come to feel that they are putting far more into the venture than they get out of it, and either want to withdraw or reserve funds for their private enjoyment. If there is a shifting pattern of personal and sexual intimacy, there may be possessiveness, jealousy and heartbreak as one liaison is replaced by another. And so on. In short, the things that make family life often difficult and taxing are likely to be not just difficult but ruinous in communal life. Virtues of a much higher order are needed for communal than for family life, and few of us are sufficiently saintly, patient or flexible to succeed at it.

Yet who knows whether, if such arrangements had been common in the community for many years, and the early education of most people included an emotional and practical preparation for that way of living, and if romantic love were not depicted in such glorious colors as it now is, communal living might become one of the attractive and practical alternatives among which people might choose?

We have been noticing ways in which it is peculiarly difficult to evaluate marriage as an institution. There is no ready way of deciding how many disadvantages are too many; and there is no very satisfactory way of assessing the merits of alternatives until they have been tried, not just in isolated cases, but widely, for a long time, and under circumstances reasonably favorable to their success.

A rather different sort of point is also important: if we notice that many more marriages than heretofore are miserable, or if it dawns on us that marriage has never been such a fine thing as it is advertised as being, it will still not be clear whether its imperfections are due to the nature of the institution, rather than being due to our want of diligence or practical wisdom in seeing to it that marriages succeed. No matter how many cases there are of dismal marriages, yours or mine need not be so, if we are primed to rely on our own resourcefulness more than on good fortune or on any supposed advantage of the institution itself.

We could sum up these deliberations by saying that the family, while a good thing in many ways or for many people, is not so unqualifiedly good as to warrant making it the only approved arrangement for conjugal living and the raising of children; and that while it is certainly good enough to be worth protecting and preserving as at least one of the standard arrangements for such purposes, it is not clear that liberal sex practices would threaten it more gravely than do the widespread violations of prohibitions of premarital and extramarital sex that have always been common. Whereas the old method of protecting marriage and the family was that of prohibiting anything else, it may be suggested that a better method might be one in which, while alternatives were treated as altogether acceptable and reputable, and hence we were left quite free to choose, (a) the merits of family life were well advertised, and (b) more effort was made to provide people with the know-how and the ambition to make marriage succeed.

What Is Love?

For ethical purposes it is not of the first importance to understand what love is; but it is a profoundly puzzling notion, and as such at least interesting to ponder. An understanding of it can have some practical consequences, particularly insofar as being in love is thought to be, at least ideally, a prerequisite of marriage.

Let us begin with a distinction between loving and being in love. While everyone who is in love loves, not everyone who loves is in love. Nearly everyone loves quite a number of people — children, brothers, sisters, grandparents, friends — but we are not in love with most of the people we love, no matter how dearly we love them. It is with persons of the opposite sex, if we are heterosexual, or of the same sex if we are not, whose age is usually close to our own, that we may be in love — at least if we ignore cases of interest to psychiatrists. Moreover, as we shall see, there is some difficulty about the concept of being in love with more than one person at once, although it will be suggested that this is not impossible.

Some of the difficulties that people often have with the notion of being in love are fairly easily removed. It need not be a problem, for example, that some people who are in love are frenzied and delirious while others are calm and tender; some are extremely possessive and others are not disturbed if their loved one also enjoys other people; some are able to love without their love being reciprocated while others can only love those who love them, and so on. This does not show either that love means different things to different people, or that it has a large variety of meanings, not all consistent with one another. To say that you are in love with someone, whatever it may be, is not to say that you are in a state of frenzy about them or that you have the tenderest of feelings toward them, even when you are in a frenzied state or do have the tenderest feelings. This is clear from the fact that if Mary asks John whether he is in love with her and he replies that he has the tenderest feelings toward her, he has stopped short of saying that he is in love.

It is not that he has not yet said enough about the state he is in. It is not that tender feelings are only one of the conditions of being in love, and Mary needs to know whether the others exist. If John went on to say that he thinks of her night and day, finds himself no longer interested in people who have formerly excited him, dotes on her every gesture and so on, he would still, no matter how long the catalogue might be, have stopped short of saying that he was in love. Nor does Mary, if she is a normal human being, know what the list should include. There is no point at which she could say, "That's enough. You are in love."

John may of course say, "I don't know what love is, but let me tell you how I feel, and perhaps you can tell me." In that case, he would not be declining to say something the significance of which he understood; but Mary could still not tell him that he was in love with her, because being in love is not a definable set of emotional qualities. What Mary should do rather, instead of listening to what he has to say about his feelings, is tell him what it means to say to someone that you are in love, and then see whether, understanding this, he can say it.

She might put it this way: telling someone you are in love with her is (in some ways) like voting, or volunteering. Another person can discuss with you how to vote or whether to volunteer, but cannot vote or volunteer for you. That you must do yourself. Similarly, telling me that you love me is a significant act that only you can perform. I can have an opinion as to whether you could sincerely do it, but nothing would be as significant for me as hearing you say it.

Mary would so far only have made the point we were making when we described John as "stopping short" of saying he was in love. She would have put it to him that it is something that he, understanding its significance, has to say; but she would not yet have explained its significance. This is a rather more difficult task, which we might approach in the following way.

An important feature of professing love is that it authorizes expectations. What these expectations are used to be clear in the days when professing love was tantamount to broaching the subject of marriage. They are no longer quite so clear, which is one of the things that makes the concept of love puzzling; but let us defer the attempt to delineate the present somewhat messy concept, in order to emphasize that it authorizes expectations, whatever exactly they may be.

Suppose that professing love were still tantamount to broaching the subject of marriage. (I speak of "broaching the subject" of marriage, rather than "proposing marriage," partly because, in the old ethic at least, only men proposed marriage, and if a woman said she was in love she would be taken to be saying that a proposal of marriage would be welcome, and partly because, even in the old days and for a man, one could profess love but decline to propose marriage if for any decent reason such as being too young, too poor or having prior obligations, marriage was not then possible. To profess love would be to say one would like to marry but . . .)

Not so long ago, then, a profession of love would entitle the loved one to expect either marriage or some reason for deferring it. It was credible that a person should be in love and decline marriage, if he were too young, too ill or already married, but not credible if the reason was lack of interest in marriage, grudging the cost of supporting a wife (in the case of a man), or being embarrassed about the "loved" one before family or friends. The person to whom love was professed would be entitled to reject reasons of the latter sort, and to expect marriage whenever reasons of the former sort no longer applied.

This needs at least one qualification: professing love is not a suitable way of broaching the subject of a marriage of convenience, or a "rational" marriage, and therefore we need to add something like that it is "ideal" (joyous, eager) marriage that is contemplated. This will also take care of the difficulty lying in the fact that the question can arise between married couples whether they still love one another. That is not just (although it is partly) a question whether they wish to continue the married state, but also a question whether they still think the state ideal. But let us concentrate on the marriage-related expectations that are authorized, remembering that we are still talking about a no longer quite accurate concept of love, and doing so to show how it authorizes expectations.

Given what we have said, clearly whether to say one is in love will be a question of whether, understanding what will be expected of us, we are prepared to live with those expectations. If we now ask, how is that question decided, the somewhat surprising answer is that we can answer it, not by examining ourselves, but by thinking about the prospect. It is not a matter of reviewing our recent history, to see such things as whether we are delighted by her presence and pained by her absence, think of her night and day, and so on, but of whether, knowing that she will expect marriage, we can bring ourselves to say the words that generate that expectation. Hence, when a person who is not being devious hesitates to profess love, that hesitation is itself the best evidence of not being in love. (Here we need to distinguish between hesitation as to what would be a propitious time for the declaration, and hesitation as to whether the declaration should be made at all.)

It might further clarify the suggestion being made here if we likened the question whether we are in love to the question whether we want to make a certain chess move. We do not decide that question by examining ourselves to see whether the desire to make that move exists, but by thinking about where the move will take us. We do not think about ourselves, but about the chess pieces and the prospects contained in the present state of the game. If, understanding the prospects and risks involved in a move, we can bring ourselves to make it, just that and no self-examination is what shows we want so to move. There are of course differences. Chess is a calculating game and love is not; but the cases are similar in that (i) professing love and making a move are both acts that get us into something; (ii) just what we get into is determined in both cases by a common understanding (in one case, of the concept of love, in the other of the rules and tactics of chess); and (iii) whether we wish so to act is determined in both cases by whether, understanding what we are getting into, we can do it.

The person who, having said various enthusiastic things, stops short of professing love, is neither confronted with the absence of a special state that we have learned to distinguish and call "love," nor with the fact that a particular assortment of thoughts, feelings or desires does not quite conform to any of the models of love, but just with the fact that he cannot bring himself to authorize the expectations contained in the common understanding of that profession. And it is not that he notices that he cannot do it, and therefore abstains. In the case of being in love, there is no observable state of inability to do something, distinct from failing to do it. This is particularly clear in the case in which he says he is in love: nothing could show the ability to do it better than the doing of it.

So far we have been concerned with how a profession of love generates expectations, and not with what expectations it generates. The older, marriage-related notion of being in love, which we took as an example because it was relatively clear-cut, is no longer quite accurate; but if the present concept of being in love is different, it will not necessarily or even likely be different in such a way as to affect our contention that love is not something we can discover by self-examination. The difference will not be in whether one is authorizing expectations by professing love but in what expectations are authorized. It is no longer clear that in the absence of serious reasons against it, marriage is to be expected of the person who goes so far as to profess love, but the changed concept could hardly fail to share important features with the older notion, otherwise one could expect a new word altogether.

What expectations are generated by the present concept? It might be anticipated, by extrapolation from the old concept, that in the absence of serious reasons against it, either marriage or cohabitation is now to be expected, given a profession of love. That is an important, if not a very interesting feature of the present concept. A more interesting feature is this (extrapolating again from the old concept): in a marriage based on love, the interests of two people become as one. They find themselves using the word "we" rather than "I" in many circumstances; for example, where questions of prudence are concerned. They may hesitate to make a large expenditure of money or of time or effort, but not because one of them begrudges it to the other. It is not so that one of them will be richer or have more leisure that the expenditure is declined, but because they think their joint time and money would be better devoted to other purposes. Two people are jointly doing just what a single person does who cannily decides on the cheaper of two pairs of shoes. This feature of the old concept still prevails in a modified form in the new: when we profess love, we can be expected to give ungrudgingly, and to treat the loved one's interests as if they were our own. This does not mean that we may not choose the cheaper of two gifts, for example, but only that we may not do so in order to reserve more money for ourselves. We may do it in order to conserve the joint wealth for what we believe to be better purposes.

We are so much in the habit of thinking of people as being ineradicably self-interested that we may have difficulty grasping this concept of the interests of two people becoming one; and yet it is an extremely common fact of experience. Husbands and wives do not normally begrudge the time, money or effort they expend in the common interest. Parents do not count the cost of clothing, feeding or educating their children; and it is a recognized application of the concept of love that whoever does begrudge these things, as distinct from being prudent in the joint interest, does not love.

To this must be added that it is only when the wish to unite one's interests with those of another person arises out of an enthusiasm for that person in particular that one is in love. In what is sometimes called a rational marriage, two people who believe in marriage but find one another no more than congenial will, as a matter of principle, subordinate their private interests to the joint interest; and although it is less likely, it is not impossible that some such relationship should emerge between people who neither marry nor live together. These are, of course, not cases of being in love, because although these people may altogether accept the primacy of the joint interest, they accept it on some principle, and not out of enthusiasm for each other.

A further feature, shared with the old concept and also connected with the notion of the primacy of the joint interest, is that the question whether one is in love is in part a question of readiness to unite oneself to one person, to the exclusion of others. This is logically connected with the primacy of the joint interest, because it is, if not impossible, at least uncommonly difficult to be related to two people at the same time in such a way that the joint interest is primary. Our present concept of being in love has not evolved because it has been found that human beings have a natural disposition to be enthusiastic about one person to the exclusion of all others. Rather, we have set it up in such a way that unless one is prepared to undertake such exclusiveness, one should not profess love.

It is often wrongly treated as a psychological question whether it is possible to be in love with two people at the same time — whether some emotional chemistry destroys one love when another comes to pass. People cite cases of one love supplanting another, and others say that while this may be the most usual effect of the emotional chemistry, it does sometimes happen that someone is boundlessly enthusiastic about two people at the same time. It is not, however, a psychological question, but a question of whether one's interests can be united simultaneously with two other people; and the peculiar difficulty of it is that my time, my affection, my productivity, however selflessly I am prepared to give them, are not, if I am in love, entirely mine to give. They belong jointly to me and another person.

To many people, it may seem perfectly obvious that it is quite impossible for anyone's interest to be jointly united with more than one person, but that may only be due to habits of thought engendered by our long history of monogamy. In a family, a joint interest relationship prevails among more than two people, and that shows that it is not impossible. Hence, perhaps this is the way it is: one of a pair of persons in love cannot unilaterally profess love to a third person without cancelling the existing relationship, because what is offered is not entirely at that person's discretion to give; but it is possible for a relationship between three or more people to come into being, in which each person is happy to share and be shared with each of the others.

The view as to the nature of love that has been outlined affects, but perhaps does not solve, a problem that may seem to arise about the connection between love and marriage. If marriage is presented to us as a lifelong affair, and we are given to understand that people ought not to embark on marriage unless they are in love, it will be natural to infer that being in love provides a strong assurance that a lifelong union will be successful; and we may well wonder what love could possibly be, to provide such an assurance, and what we can look for in ourselves that would show conclusively whether we are in this extraordinary state.

The answers are that it is a misconception that love offers high assurance that marriage will be successful, and that there is nothing we might look for in ourselves that will show that a marriage we undertake is likely to succeed.

It is not difficult to understand how one could want to unite oneself with another person in such a way that the joint interest is primary, as long as nothing is specified as to the duration of the union, but it is quite difficult to understand how such a union could seriously be desired when it is meant to be for any length of time longer than the foreseeable future — for ten years, say, or for the rest of one's life. People are notoriously liable to discover profoundly unsatisfactory things about one another in the course of living together, or to affect one another in such a way that each becomes quite a different person, or to change as a result of other influences and developments in their lives, or to find themselves immensely more interested in some other person. If marriage vows included the words "for as long as we both shall love," there would be no problem; but containing as they do the words "for as long as we both shall live," it is difficult to see how anyone could ever decide whether to marry.

Whether we want the joint responsibility of marriage is not shown by any kind of self-examination, but by whether, clearly understanding what is proposed, we can cheerfully embark on it; and the fact that we cheerfully embark on it does not itself have any tendency to show that we will continue to be cheerful about it a year or forty years hence.

The tendency to suppose that if two people are genuinely in love that alone will assure a lasting and a good marriage is undoubtedly responsible for some of the difficulties that people encounter in marriage. Many couples have no doubt whatever that they are in love; and if they also believe that to be in love is to be assured of a happy marriage, they will rely too much on this magic to make their marriage work, and will not be prepared for the intelligence, flexibility, patience and persistence needed over the long haul.

In this chapter we began by raising some questions as to the possibilities of moral fault when we make love. In doing so we provisionally set aside the question whether one might be at fault just through making love outside of marriage; and we found that, apart from any moral objection there might be on those grounds, while there were various different ways in which we clearly could go wrong, still with a little honesty, concern for other people, and perhaps good fortune, it is not so very difficult to avoid causing harm or being unfair, cruel, selfish or deceitful in one's sex life.

In the second part of the chapter we turned to the questions provisionally set aside in the first, as to moral claims on us arising from the monogamous principle. The general conclusion we reached was that, while it may be admirable to choose to live according to the monogamous principle, there is no adequate reason for requiring everyone to accept it. There is much to be said in favor of marriage, but it does not emerge either as the only good way of arranging conjugal living or the care of the young, or so very much superior to other imaginable ways as to warrant treating all others as wrong, rather than as sometimes (in some circumstances, or for some people) less to be recommended than marriage.

A general suggestion was that marriage might best be treated not as a moral requirement, but as an option, one about which some of us might be very enthusiastic, and that we would recommend very highly to our children or our friends, but that would be treated even so as something desirable, rather than as something morally necessary. If this suggestion were adopted, even the most enthusiastic proponents of marriage would treat it as wise, rather than saintly, to marry, and sad, rather than sinful, not to. Perhaps, however, everyone would treat it as sinful, having married, to be remiss in the execution of what one has thereby undertaken.

Whether or not one accepts the monogamous principle, it is hard to deny that there are happy and rewarding marriages, or even to deny that a marriage that is currently joyless may, with good management or good fortune, turn out successfully. Hence there is not much room for dispute as to whether an action that destroys or adversely affects an otherwise good marriage, or adversely affects the chances of a poor marriage improving, is morally faulty. Some love affairs have such effects; and if they do, or if they fail to do so only by the sheerest good fortune, they are morally irresponsible; but love affairs between unmarried persons are very unlikely to fall into this category, and not every sexual entangelement between a marriage partner and a third party has, or even threatens to have such effects.

The remaining moral questions in the case of such entangle-ments are whether deception is necessary, and whether a vow is broken. We have shown that deception is not always necessary in order to avoid adverse effects and that in our culture it is regretta-bly not very clear how seriously marriage vows need to be taken, especially if in breaking them one is not being dishonest, unfair, selfish or cruel.

Hence the conclusions of the first part of this chapter do not need to be fundamentally revised in the light of claims upon us of the monogamous principle, at least if, as we suggested, those claims are better treated as recommendations than as moral re-quirements. Our sex lives need not, and very often will not, adversely affect either the prospects of our own marriage being a good one, or the success of other people's marriages.

Lots of us may be delighted to hear such tidings, and may not stay for the further point that while our sex lives need not and often will not have such effects, still they may, and when they do, or when they are likely to, that is a matter of quite serious moral concern.

THREE

Sex and Personal Intimacy

We have found that while our sex lives are matters of proper moral concern in many ways and cases, sexual activity is not immoral nearly so often as some people would have us believe. In this chapter it will be suggested that there is more than one mode of evaluation of behavior in general and sexual behavior in particular: not all defects are moral imperfections, and not all perfections moral virtues. The specific mode of evaluation with which we will be concerned here is that of personal intimacy. What we will call "personal intimacy" is not something commonly known by that or any other name; but it will be argued that it is something about which many people do care, and which could be recommended to those who so far have not learned to care about it.

Before explaining the concept of personal intimacy, it will be useful to make as clear as possible the idea, and the implications of the idea, that there are various modes of evaluation of behavior, not all of them moral. That will be the task of this Introduction.

We may praise or criticize human behavior on moral, aesthetic and intellectual grounds, to name some of the most obvious. People are admired for achieving high standards, and criticized for failing to do so, but the admiration and criticism are of a different kind from case to case. Except in special cases, it is not immoral to paint a picture amateurishly or sing a tune off key. We would criticize but not deplore these things, and certainly not chastize or imprison the person who did them.

We admire people who are witty, perceptive, friendly or warm, and criticize them for being humorless or obtuse or insensitive; but except in special cases, the former are not moral virtues and the latter not moral vices. It is not saintly of a person to be an entertaining conversationalist or a shrewd observer; it is possible for thieves, liars, and cowards to be perceptive or witty and for honest, brave and generous people to be dull, gauche or unfriendly.

There is disagreement among philosophers as to what exactly is the mark of a specifically *moral* criticism. This question should not be confused with the question of what in particular is good or bad, right or wrong — a question about which there is also disagreement, and not only amongst philosophers. We disagree about whether drinking and gambling and prostitution are wrong; but we are faced with quite a different sort of disagreement when we are agreed that something is defective, not to be recommended or deserving of criticism, but not agreed as to what *kind* of defect it has or what kind of criticism it deserves. Two people might agree, for example, that gambling is best avoided, but disagree as to whether it is immoral, or merely imprudent. Or again, they might agree that there is something substandard about an ostensibly amiable relationship between persons between whom there is no genuine good feeling — the kind of relationship that sometimes exists between businessmen who cultivate the friendships of persons who will turn business their way — but disagree as to whether the agreed imperfection is a moral fault.

These disagreements are often difficult to handle, partly because it is not always clear what is at issue, and partly because, since they arise less frequently than others, we have less chance to acquire skill in discussing them. Yet they may be of considerable importance. The person who believes gambling to be imprudent may perhaps counsel others against it, pointing out its dangers, but will leave it up to them whether, understanding what they are getting into, they do it; but the person who thinks it immoral may be reluctant to associate with anyone who gambles, and may support the enactment or the continuance in force of laws making gambling a criminal offence.

The word "moral" may confuse us here, because it seems to be used in one way when we ask whether something is a moral, an aesthetic, a prudential or some other kind of question, and in a different way when we ask whether an action is moral or immoral. Perhaps it is more accurate to say that, oddly enough, "moral" is not the opposite of "immoral." "Immoral" has a meaning like "wicked," but "moral" does not have a meaning like "virtuous." Questions, arguments and anxieties are describable as being moral, meaning that they have to do with good *and* evil, virtue *and* vice; but if a person is described as being moral, it is by no means clear what is meant. We would have to ask whether the speaker meant "virtuous," or "particularly concerned about questions of right and wrong," or "inclined to reprove and blame" or what?

Our question then is what makes a criticism or a commendation moral, as distinct from prudential, aesthetic or anything else; and we might not be far from the truth if we said something like this: whereas it is merely welcome if a person has such qualities as wit, charm or skill, and regrettable if he lacks them, a moral virtue is one that we *require* of a person, and a moral defect is one that we regard ourselves as having a right to complain of. If we mention to a person that he is dull or gauche, we do so apologetically. We do not accuse him of it, as if it were something he ought to have known better than to be. If, however, we believe that a person has been treacherous or cruel, then while we may out of fear or for other reasons decline to say anything about it, if we do say anything we will say it accusingly, representing the defect as something unacceptable, something that must be corrected.

The point is sharply illustrated by the case of criminal behavior, which can be regarded as a sub-species of immoral behavior. If someone performs a criminal act, although we may be given some psychiatric explanation that makes us regard his behavior as excusable, and therefore not punish him, we will still want to insist or even ensure that he cease performing acts of that kind. The excuse does not make the action permissible, or make it a matter for his discretion whether he performs such acts in future. Excusable or not, we are not prepared to tolerate such acts.

Criminal acts are a comparatively small subset of immoral acts, but the same principle can be seen to apply to the whole range of immoral behavior; that is, that an action is not immoral if it is not at least regarded as unacceptable, no matter by whom it is performed, or for what reasons. If an objectionable action is of a comparatively unimportant kind, as is cheating in a friendly game of cards, we may think it best not to raise objections and complaints, but we do not therefore regard it as acceptable. If, whether grave or not, the action is excusable as having been done in the heat of passion or in ignorance or by mistake, it is again still not regarded as therefore permissible. We would still urgently do whatever we could to discourage its repetition.

An exercise that might serve as a test of whether a defective action is immoral rather than defective in some other way is to consider whether if, instead of our police courts and prisons we had an electronic system of monitoring and punishing wrongdoing — a system that was fast, inexpensive, efficient and just — we would care to program the system to monitor the action in question. If we would not want to program it to monitor sitting in drafts, making dull conversation or buying a used car from a disreputable dealer, that would indicate that we do not regard these acts, however regrettable, as being immoral; while if we were quite ready to program it to handle insulting remarks, cheating at cards or jilting one's girlfriend, that would indicate that these acts, however unimportant, were regarded as unacceptable and immoral.

The distinction is obscured by our belief in tolerance, because we often do not object to things we nevertheless regard as unacceptable. Few people are quite clear about whether being tolerant involves not having moral convictions, or just not being disagreeable about them; nor are many of us clear about whether it is a virtue to be tolerant about everything, or just about some things. It is one thing to be tolerant of unimportant defects, or in matters about which there can be honest moral disagreement, and another to be tolerant in matters about which disagreement is scarcely possible, and which are important. If I support a certain political party out of moral conviction, I may still recognize that it is possible to support a different party for moral reasons, and hence not want to charge any and every supporter of other parties with moral defect; and if I disapprove of my friend's abrasive manner toward anyone he thinks foolish, I may feel it is not important enough to make a fuss over. But if someone poisons his grandmother I can neither regard the matter as unimportant nor entertain the possibility of there being honest disagreement about its wrongness, and it is hard to see tolerance as still being a virtue in that case.

To be tolerant does not mean having no standards to apply to oneself or other people. On the contrary, the idea of tolerance logically requires that there should be something to be tolerated. One cannot tolerate something one does not find regrettable. If I disapprove of gambling but you do not, I can be tolerant of it, but you cannot. Nor can you be intolerant.

Being tolerant is declining to make a fuss over things one finds in some degree deplorable; and it can be recommended as a policy only (a) with respect to actions that are relatively unimportant, or (b) with respect to actions about whose morality honest people can disagree, or (c) in cases in which making a fuss is likely to do more harm than good.

There is another distinction here that is not always appreciated: that between objecting in a heated, indignant or vituperative way, and doing so with restraint, and respectfully. The former is both disagreeable and, most often, counter-productive, and is therefore abhorred; but the choice is not between objecting in *that* kind of way and not objecting at all; and tolerance is quite consistent with objecting restrainedly and respectfully.

We can have difficulty seeing that what makes a criticism moral, rather than aesthetic or prudential, is its being regarded as something on which we have a right to insist, if either we (wrongly) think that tolerance requires not having standards, or if the case is one in which one might (tolerantly) not in fact complain. It could still be the mark of a specifically moral criticism that *if* it were to be made, it would be represented as requiring something of a person.

It is worth repeating that we must not confuse a test of whether a criticism is specifically moral with a test of whether an action is right or wrong. The test we have offered is a way of deciding into what category a criticism falls, but within a given category the tests of merit and defect will be of a different sort. We could not decide whether something was immoral by whether we saw ourselves as having a right to object to it: we would not know whether we had that right until we knew whether it was immoral. The music teacher who is indignant about his student's piano playing thereby shows perhaps that he conceives it to be immoral to play imperfectly; but whether it *is* immoral depends, not on whether he is indignant, but on whether the defective performance is dishonest, unfair, cruel, selfish, cowardly or dangerous.

The distinction we have been making opens the possibility that some of our sexual activities may be regrettable without being immoral; but if anything is substandard in some nonmoral way, its avoidance will not be something we have a right to require of people, but will be a matter of preference, recommendation, encouragement. We will perhaps teach people to appreciate the preferred way of managing things, in much the way we cultivate taste in architecture or music. The preferred way will be recommended, not as a concession to other people, but primarily as something personally rewarding; and it will be treated as sad, rather than unacceptable, when anyone is slow to learn such things.

WHAT IS PERSONAL INTIMACY?

There are at least three distinguishable ways in which personal relations can be better or worse, and it will be the aim of this section to concentrate on one of these, delineating it as clearly as possible and distinguishing it from the other two.

We might call the first point of view from which our relations with people can be evaluated that of *congeniality*. If two people bore or annoy one another, then given that they have a relationship —

for example, if they work at the same place or are members of the same family — it is a poor or unsatisfactory one; while if each finds the other amusing, interesting or merely agreeable, they have a satisfactory or congenial relationship. If they are uncongenial they may also be nasty or deceitful, and then their relationship will involve questions of morality; but an uncongenial relationship is not in itself immoral, nor is a congenial one in itself virtuous. We can be uncongenial without being nasty, and congenial without being helpful or considerate. There is, of course, the case in which it is because someone is immoral in some way that he is uncongenial; but even here there is a distinction between the person interesting enough to be congenial, if he were not so malicious, and the person who would be boring even if he were saintly.

Secondly, a person can be morally upright in his dealings with people, without finding those persons congenial or being found so by them. Indeed, we might say that it is the mark of a virtuous person to be honest, generous and so on toward others regardless of whether they are congenial. A person who is fair or considerate only toward people he likes is to that extent morally defective.

Congeniality and morality are then two of our three ways in which personal relationships can be better or worse; and their distinctness from one another is shown by their independent variability, by the fact that one of them can exist without the other.

The third dimension we will call *personal intimacy*. That expression has no clear ordinary use, nor do we have much else in the way of a standard vocabulary for talking about this quality sometimes found in our relations with people; however, if we describe some examples of its presence and its absence, most of us will recognize something that we care a good deal about; that we rejoice in when it exists and regret when it does not exist.

If two people see a good deal of one another, talk animatedly and enjoy doing things together, each may yet remain somewhat of a mystery to the other. An amusing remark about a serious subject may leave the other person wondering whether the remark was made with no serious intent and merely because it was amusing, or whether it expressed a cynical or sceptical attitude. If questions like that somehow just cannot be raised between them, their relationship may be felt to be defective in being, although extremely congenial, quite superficial.

Similarly, if two people have been on friendly terms and one of them moves to another city for a time and does not write, but resumes the amicable relationship on his return, it may be unclear whether in the interval he missed or thought about his friend, or whether the friendship had no deeper basis than the pleasure of the moment. If that question could somehow not be raised, then although these two people may entirely enjoy one another, and although there need be no deception, unkindness or other moral fault, something is missing.

It is the same thing as is missing sometimes between persons who meet and have a convivial time at a party. They may regard party conversation as a kind of game at which one can be skilled, the object of which is to take on any topic someone raises and make it the subject of a fine display of wit and discernment. Part of the fun is in being able to do something with whatever topic comes up, and poor players are people who are stumped by too many topics. One may very much enjoy this game, and be delighted to meet someone who plays it well, but go away knowing little about the other person, not interested in how he gets along with his wife, what he does on weekends or whether he fears death, and not inclined to help him fix his washing machine or to drop by his place on a Saturday just to say hello. It is not that in party conversation such personal topics as the fear of death are avoided, but they are treated in a way that leaves it unclear what lies behind the display of wit and discernment: whether the good conversationalist has the same thoughts when he is alone at night as he is now offering for our amusement.

We might say that in such cases what is missing is interest in the person. There is interest, not in the person, but in the output: in various capacities that we may find amusing or congenial or useful. We may want good company or good conversation or skill at chess or tennis or lovemaking, and it may not matter who possesses these desired qualities.

We see the same lack of personal interest in commercial relationships, although in these cases it does not usually strike anyone as regrettable. A plumber comes and fixes the water tank; we pay him and he rushes on to his next job. There is perhaps time for a joke or for him to admire the garden, but there is little question of his staying for supper. We are interested in him only in his capacity as a fixer of pipes. This is not because of snobbishness about plumbers: it would be the same with lawyers or doctors. There is just not time in our lives for more than a few close personal relationships.

We should not let the examples of the plumber or the party-goer lead us to think that it is a question of *how many* of a person's capacities we are interested in. Two people may be married and find one another satisfactory mates. They may usually sort out their differences amicably, be proud of one another in public, have interesting conversations about friends, films and books, and enjoy one another in bed—and yet be quite capable of parting with no greater sense of loss than derives from the rarity of such a congenial arrangement. If one mate could immediately be replaced by another equally congenial and there was no sense of a particular personal loss, then there was not an attachment to just this person. Each person was interested, not in the other person, but in that person's conversation, taste, cheerfulness, cooking ability or sexual compatibility.

This extreme case brings out an important point about the concept of being interested in specific persons. As long as we limit ourselves to cases in which we are interested in some one or some few qualities in a person, it can look as if what is missing is just breadth of appreciation: if we were interested in a person not only as an enjoyable lover or a competent plumber or an agreeable conversationalist, but in most of his other qualities and abilities as well, that would be what it is to be interested in him as a person. But in the case of the couple who are entirely pleased with one another, there are no other qualities to be appreciated. Hence the question arises, what is it to be interested in a person? What can there be, over and above all the qualities we are supposing these two people appreciate, in which they might be interested? It would surely be absurd to say that we are interested in something that never shows, something underlying all such things as high spirits and courage and gentleness and wit.

If we seem here to be on the verge of having to suppose that there is something mysterious or hidden that we can appreciate or fail to appreciate, it is perhaps because we are predisposed to think that being interested in a person is a matter of appreciating some good quality or another. Given that supposition, on the one hand, we must find some quality to be appreciated, and on the other, in the case of the couple who like most everything about one another, we can find no ordinary quality to fill the slot, and we have no option but to look for some mysterious or hidden quality. But if being interested in someone is not a matter of appreciating qualities, we will not find ourselves in that peculiar fix.

What then *is* being interested in a person? If we suppose that there is nothing mysterious about it, it ought to be accessible to perceptive observation. As a prelude to trying to say what it is, let us review some significant differences we can notice between personal and impersonal relationships. To do this we can either set before ourselves some extreme cases, or construct a composite out of tendencies noticeable in various moderate cases.

1. The conversation of people whose relation is impersonal will have a kind of showiness about it, as if they were always playing to an audience; and the topics of conversation will either run to matters of little or no personal involvement, such as films, books, news items, puzzles and scientific curiosities, or, if they extend to such things as the hopes, fears, joys and tribulations of the parties themselves, will be handled in such a way as to conceal attitudes. A

person will perhaps be amusing or scientific about his fears, and one will be left wondering whether he is amused by them when they are upon him, and if so what kind of fears they can be.

2. In an impersonal relation, each person's appreciation of the other will run noticeably to concentration on the output, as we have put it: on the joke or the interesting story, for example, rather than on who made the joke or told the story. It is the difference between "What a good joke!" and "How funny you are!" Each will rejoice in the interest of the performance, and it will seem incidental who is performing.

3. In an impersonal relation, tensions, disagreements, and disappointments will tend immediately to threaten the connection. If we are interested only in the quality of the output, enthusiasm will diminish to the extent that the quality deteriorates. The attitude will be like the average person's feeling for his car: delighted with it as long as it looks good and performs well, willing to put up with it when it develops faults as long as no other is readily available, and able to part with it without a sigh when something better becomes available.

4. By contrast, we tend to dote even on the imperfections of someone in whom our interest is personal. The peculiar plainness of a face or a peculiar awkwardness of manner are welcomed, not as being in general admirable qualities, but just as being so characteristic of a person for whom we care.

5. While people who are impersonally related may stimulate each other to better than average displays of their capabilities, when a relation is personal we draw each other out, reveal ourselves. We express ourselves unreservedly to one another, and if there is uncertainty as to the other person's attitudes or feelings, it is not because they are kept back, but just because there has not happened to be an occasion to express them.

From these observations we might construct the following generalizations:

- A test of whether a relationship is personal or not is whether anyone else having the same or comparable good qualities would do as well. A commercial relationship is usually impersonal, and there it makes no difference, as between honest and competent practitioners, whom we employ; and similarly in our friendships if we can move without a sigh from one person to another who is equally congenial, our relationship is impersonal.

- The application of this test is complicated somewhat by the fact that it may pain us to lose a friend, not because of a particular attachment to that person, but only because congenial connections can be somewhat rare, or because we have been particularly fortunate in a certain friendship. Then we will experience a sense of loss, and it may not be clear whether that is because there was a particular attachment, or because of the difficulty of finding a replacement. The test may still be useful, however, either in the case in which we are fortunate in replacing one friend by another, or in the case in which, although we enjoyed a friendship and it was not replaced by another, no loss was felt. In other cases, we may have to apply other tests.

- There is, paradoxically perhaps, a sense in which a personal relation is objective, and an impersonal one subjective: in the latter case it is just to the extent that I find a person's qualities agreeable or congenial that I am interested, whereas in the former case I care about a person's tastes or hopes or fears *whatever they may be*, just because they are that person's. There is thus a quality of total acceptance about a relationship that is personal, a readiness to let the chips fall where they may.

- There are two related character traits that make for personal intimacy, one a disposition to trust other people, so that one will not fear to reveal oneself, and the other a tendency to inspire trust. Conversely, a disposition to fear other people and a tendency to inspire fear will make for such self-concealing behavior as hiding behind a wall of banter and wit, or avoiding such closeness as would create pressures to show oneself.

Being interested in a person, then, is not a matter of appreciating something in addition to various charms and abilities, but of relating to someone in a certain way — a way that is outgoing and trusting, that is not contingent on maintaining any particular standard of attractiveness or agreeability, and that tends to find personal qualities interesting independent of their charm, just because they are the qualities of a given person.

To make perfectly clear that personal intimacy is a quality of human relationships quite distinct from morality or congeniality, we need to show that it varies independently of them, that whatever connections there may be, it is possible to have one without the other.

In the case of congeniality, there is a connection with personal intimacy in that we are not likely to have a very close relationship with someone who is quite uncongenial; but on the other hand, (a) the person with an aptitude for personal intimacy will be undemanding with regard to congeniality, will not always be reviewing friendships as to whether they are sufficiently rewarding; and (b) clearly there is congeniality without personal intimacy in our cases of the party-goers or the couple who find one another altogether agreeable.

In the case of morality, it seems clear in the first place that there need be nothing morally wrong with a relationship that is impersonal. Take, as the hardest case, the man who engages the services of a prostitute: there need be nothing deceitful, cruel, unfair, selfish or cowardly about such an episode, and hence except in special cases his action, although impersonal, is not immoral. There can, of course, be immorality in such cases; for example, if he is cruel or gratuitously insulting to the woman, or does not pay her, or if he later has sexual contact with someone else without knowing whether he has contracted venereal disease, or if he pretends to deplore the practice of prostitution. But none of these faults must exist, and when they do not it is difficult to see on what ground it could be represented as immoral to use the services of a prostitute. Yet the relationship is normally lacking in personal warmth.

(There is something to be said for the argument that, since it is almost certainly harmful to a person, at least over any length of time, to be a prostitute, anyone employing her services contributes to the degradation of a human being. To do that is certainly immoral; but since prostitutes will generally continue their activities regardless of whether any particular person employs them, it is not perfectly clear whether each customer contributes to their degradation. But even if that is true, it is not because the relationship is impersonal that something immoral is done, but because the life of a prostitute is so afflicted with cruelty, harassment and disease.)

Take a less extreme case: there are people who do not much care for other people, but greatly enjoy the excitement of sex. They may seek out others who are like-minded, and who when called upon most any time will eagerly make love. If these people conscientiously avoid sexual involvement with anyone who shows signs of being in love, or of regarding sexual activity as anything more than a pleasure, and if they are careful not to mislead another person as to their own attitude, there would be nothing dishonest, cruel, harmful or unfair about their practice, and therefore no ground for saying it is immoral. However, such relationships are clearly impersonal.

This is not to say, of course, that no purely sexual relationship is ever immoral, but only that it is not immoral just because it is purely sexual. If there is deception or cruelty, or carelessness about contraception, there will be moral defect; but those faults are independent of the impersonal character of the relationship, and by no means typical of such relationships.

At the other extreme from our first case is the example of our broadly congenial couple whose relation is impersonal. It is obvious here that in spite of the impersonal character of their relationship, there is nothing immoral about it. They may be as fair, honest, generous and considerate as anyone could ask, without revealing themselves to one another, or having any greater attachment than is dictated by the quality of the other person's charms.

Yet there are two reasons why, in spite of the above arguments, some people might hesitate to accept the contention that morality varies independently of personal intimacy:

1. Morality is often (and probably correctly) represented as being at least in part a matter of respect for persons, of treating other people, as Kant put it, "never merely as means, but always also as ends in themselves"; but personal intimacy appears from what we have seen to require the same attitude. How then is it possible for them to vary independently?

The answer is that the ethical way of treating people as ends in themselves is different from the personal intimacy way. A typical ethical application of the principle might be that if something one considers doing will adversely affect another person, then that fact alone demands to be taken account of in our ethical thinking. The ethical attitude is that it does not matter whether the person in question is a friend or a stranger, rich or poor, saintly or sinful. All we need to know is that a human being would be adversely affected. To have that attitude is to have respect for persons. If I delude someone, even into doing something that is to his advantage, I have not treated him with the kind of respect due to a person: I have not allowed him to decide in a free and well-informed way what he will do. In these cases, it is just because it is a human being we are dealing with that we act in certain ways, not because it is a specific person. It may be a boring and annoying fact that his interests would be adversely affected. We need not be intrigued by it or probe into it; and our actions can be affected by it without there being any personal contact whatever, without the other person knowing that we have changed our plans because of the way they might affect his interests. He can be someone we know of only indirectly; and even where there is personal contact, the transaction need involve none of the colorful interplay between persons that is characteristic of personal intimacy.

In the moral application of the principle, whether we are interested in a person or not, we treat him with respect; whereas the application in the case of personal intimacy is a matter of taking an interest. The interest we take is itself the burden of the principle. We take that interest, not with a view to being able to behave well toward other people, but with a view to appreciating them more, and to having a warmer and richer relationship.

2. It is sometimes said that a person is morally defective if he does right by other people merely from principle, and not out of any kind of affection or personal concern. If this is true, then personal intimacy would perhaps have to be regarded as part of morality, and they could not vary independently; but surely it is not true. A wife may be disappointed if her husband is faithful and considerate, not out of enthusiasm for her, but out of duty, but she can hardly say it is morally defective of him. She is right in thinking that it would be more rewarding if he rejoiced in her as a person, but wrong in thinking it would be morally better. She has not made the distinction we have been trying to draw between two fundamentally different types or scales of evaluation.

Morality requires that we do right by people regardless of whether we know or like them, and therefore it must vary independently of personal intimacy. The quality of life would deteriorate radically if we were expected to be fair or generous only to our friends.

There are, however, relations between the personal and the ethical. Although it is possible to treat another person fairly and with consideration when one feels no personal attachment or enthusiasm, it requires a particular effort and a higher level of concern than is common in the human race. On the other hand, it comes naturally to us to be fair and considerate to someone we rejoice in as a person, because when we care for a person, we become involved in their interests as if they were our own.

In such relations as these between the personal and the moral lies the great strength of any moral perspective in which love has a central place; for example, Christianity. It is easy and natural to do right by someone you love; and one might say that Christianity, recognizing this, chooses to say little about just how to do right, but instead tries to encourage love, which may, if we independently have some understanding of moral virtue, motivate us to do what we know to be right. The weaknesses of such an approach are chiefly two: (i) it tends not to face up to the fact that, while we must do right by everyone, we deceive ourselves if we think we can or do love everyone, and (ii) it offers little guidance as to how to do right, and thus both leaves us ill equipped for the finer questions of right behavior toward those we do love, and quite unprepared for virtuous treatment of people we do not love. It also encourages us to believe that we love people whom we do not love, and so to believe that we are doing right by them when we are not.

If we are right in concluding that it is not a moral question whether our relations with other people are impersonal, then given what we said in the Introduction to this chapter, impersonal relationships are not something we have a right to complain of, and personal intimacy is not something we have a right to insist on. If I choose to avoid people who, however amusing they may be, do not reveal themselves and take no personal interest in me, I am expressing a personal preference. I should not despise or deplore such people, and there should be no question of their being penalized or refused entry into the country, as there might be if they were deemed immoral.

If it is not a moral question what kind of personal relationships we have, but a matter of personal preference, is it as much a matter of taste as whether one likes strawberry jam, or are there nonmoral considerations that make one kind of relationship preferable to another?

To put the question just this way suggests falsely that personal intimacy can be achieved at will, that it is as much under our control as what we eat or what we do with our leisure time. There are at least two reasons why this is not true: (i) it is a mutual thing, and depends very much on the reactions and attitudes of the other person, and (ii) one has to have or to cultivate a certain disposition before it is possible, and when one has that disposition, close personal relationships *happen,* rather than being artfully brought about. One cannot turn on the trust, the demonstrativeness or the kind of "objective" interest in people that we described earlier. If it is turned on, either its artificiality shows, defeating one's purpose, or in any case it *is* artificial, and a falsity in the relationship emerges.

Yet it may be possible over a period of time to cultivate these qualities in oneself; and for that reason it is worth asking what sorts of personal relations are preferable. As with most questions of personal preference, the considerations making something advisable or otherwise will relate to individual tastes, capacities and situations, and therefore the wisest and best advised will not necessarily all make the same choice. Some people may be constitutionally ill equipped for close personal relations, and may be happier emphasizing other forms of social relationship. However, since we are all capable of changing, it is difficult to be sure what one's taste or capacity is. Just as a person who initially dislikes chess or mathematics may become an enthusiast, so we may initially derive little satisfaction from friendships, until perhaps some exceptional person breaks through the barriers of reserve and awkwardness and shows us capacities we did not know we had.

What kind of personal relations are preferable is perhaps basically a question of whether one finds a certain picture of oneself acceptable. One can live for a long time without self-examination, but when attention is drawn to the fact that in a sense one's life is perfectly solitary, that other people are nothing but sources of pleasure or annoyance, it is a question whether that fact is disturbing.

It is important here to keep moral considerations out of it. It is not a question of selfishness. It is possible to be quite generous and considerate of other people while taking no interest in them as persons. We should focus on the solitude and egoism of someone of as much moral rectitude as one could wish, who however takes no interest in people except insofar as either duty requires or fancy dictates.

We must all decide for ourselves whether we can live with such a picture of ourselves; but it is evident that many people neither want it for themselves nor like it in other people. This shows in their dismay at the coldness of someone who, however entertainingly, talks at them rather than to them, who loses interest if he is not entertained in return, who shows no curiosity about their hopes and anxieties, and with whom friendship seems a very fragile thing, entirely dependent on maintaining a sufficiently amusing output. It shows also in the desire of many people to reveal themselves: to be demonstrative in the expression of feeling, to share their dreams, discuss their problems or make known their virtues and faults.

We are in many ways afraid of other people, afraid of boring them or appearing foolish, afraid of establishing relationships that may overwhelm or hurt us, and so we withdraw behind facades of manners and safe behavior. But at the same time many of us yearn for warmer and more open personal relationships, and find it immensely gratifying if, with some few persons, this can be achieved.

It might be possible to see more clearly why personal intimacy can be gratifying if we paused here to replace a possible misconception as to its nature with a more revealing understanding of it. We sometimes want very much to be close to another person: to trust, to understand, to share secrets, to know that nothing is held back, and to be confident that if we express ourselves freely, what we say and do will be rejoiced in. While many of us want this, for some of us its achievement is a rare turn of fortune, and most of the time with most people we feel a lack of such intimacy. We are unsure whether we enjoy the confidence of another person, wonder what that person's real thoughts or feelings are, hesitate to let ourselves go for fear of doing or saying unwelcome things.

At such times another person may seem a mystery to us, something concealed behind actions and words, deep inside. It can seem that it is this inner person that we yearn to know; and when we reflect that we can never see behind a person's actions and words, we can come to feel unbearably alone in the world. The inner person is there, we think, but can never be known. Yet the idea of knowing the inner person does not cease to attract us. Any kind of closeness seems to be an approach to it, and it can even seem disappointing that by gazing into someone's eyes we cannot see the soul that lies behind them. Sexual intimacy similarly seems a way of getting close, and this may be one source of the intensity of our interest in sex; but again it is maddening that even here the hidden person is still not revealed.

It can seem to us that people's natures are very imperfectly shown by the way they smile, the things they say, the things that make them angry or sad or jubilant. We are impatient with the (as it seems) crude indications of the real person that we find in smiles and jokes and fits of temper, and we wish we could see right into a person. We of course do not want to see the inner things a surgeon sees, but rather the contents of another person's consciousness. We reckon that a person's true thoughts, desires, hopes and fears appear undisguised on the inner stage of consciousness, and it is for that show that we would like to have tickets.

Yet when we think of it, it should strike us that we do not know *ourselves* the way we would like to know another person. If we concentrate our attention just on what we are conscious of over any randomly chosen interval of time, the show is disappointing: perhaps some feelings of heat or cold, a twinge of pain in the shoulder, a sensation in the throat as we breathe, a slight feeling of weariness, a stray thought here and there about a problem that worries us or a plan we have. Nothing very significant or very revealing. If we could chronicle accurately what we are conscious of over any period of time, even the time when we are doing something that leaves another person mystified, it would be an uninteresting catalogue, and would scarcely satisfy anyone's desire to know the person behind our words and deeds. The fact, however, that the contents of anyone's consciousness are uninteresting does not show that we are all uninteresting people. A person may deliver himself of all sorts of ingenious suggestions, shrewd observations, beguiling fancies and comical remarks, and be most unusual in the things that excite or sadden him, without his conscious states being interesting to know of. The dullest and most interesting people will not likely differ greatly in the true reports they make of their conscious states.

If this seems surprising to you, perhaps that is because you think that everything of which a person delivers himself first appears on the inner stage; that only some of the things that so appear are in fact delivered; and that often what appears inwardly differs from what is delivered, owing either to some want of skill in expressing thoughts, feelings and attitudes, or to some reserve or some deviousness that makes us falsify what we say about ourselves.

If that were the case, there would be much more on the inner stage than is ever revealed outwardly, and in knowing the happenings on the inner stage one would be knowing a person as he is and not as he pretends to be or, through ineptitude, falsely appears to be. Yet are there always two things going on, what we think and what we say; and is it the case that these two things sometimes (perhaps ideally) agree, but all too often differ, either in that we say much less than we think, or in that we say something different from what we think?

Catch yourself in a lively and friendly conversation with someone and you will find that for the most part you just say things: you do not first think them and then say them, but interesting, funny or instructive remarks come forth directly. What you say is, even for you, all there is to your part of the conversation. It does not even *seem* as if something inward showed you what to say, and then you said it.

If the conversation is about a difficult or unfamiliar topic, the flow may not be so smooth. You may have to stop and struggle to find words. You may experience a sense of tension and effort, and may inwardly formulate something to say and decide against saying it because it is not quite true or not sufficiently clear; but if you find the right thing to say you will not generally say it to yourself first, and then aloud: after a time, words will come, and when you have said them you may or may not be pleased with the result of your struggle.

If a conversation is delicate and requires diplomacy, you may find yourself saying something different from what you think; but what you think is not necessarily or even generally spoken inwardly prior to or alongside of what you say: it is just that if you asked yourself whether what you said was quite frank, you would have to say no. What you said aloud is different, not from what you said inwardly, but from what you would have said had you not been moved by diplomatic considerations.

Is this diplomacy at least something that went on inwardly, concealed from the other person — something that, had he seen it in the flow of your consciousness, he would have found revealing or disappointing? Perhaps some people think out their diplomatic stratagems explicitly, saying to themselves, for example, "I had better say something complimentary to this chap, because he is so sensitive"; but generally a diplomatic person acts instinctively. The artful things he says are not premeditated, but are a direct or prime expression of his sensitivity to another person's fears or foibles. Diplomacy then is not a secret process but a personal trait of certain individuals that is usually quite apparent.

Sometimes a person who knows a great deal about some subject, when talking to a beginner, will say much less than he knows; but the things he knows and does not say are not things that run through his head at such times and are not made public, but rather things he has learned and now could say, if he were talking to someone to whom they would be intelligible or useful.

Through these various cases, we can see that there is something right about the idea that what a person says may be the same as or different from what he thinks; but we go wrong if we imagine that what he thinks is something that goes on prior to or alongside of what he says, and that therefore it would be useful to be able to see into his consciousness. When a person is being frank, he indeed says what he thinks, but that just means that he is not being diplomatic or devious, that he would say the same to his diary or anyone else. When a person is being diplomatic he may say something different from what he thinks, but that just means that what he would write in his diary or say to someone else would not square with what he diplomatically said. When a person explains something to a beginner he tells less than he knows, but that just means that if he were writing a book, he would without further research have a great deal more to say. What is more than or different from what people say is not something that is there but hidden, something that would be fully revealed if only we could see into people's minds, but something they might have said, or done, had circumstances been different.

The things we might do or say, the things we are capable of, the poems we could write, the fun we might concoct, the sympathy or courage we might show, are in a sense hidden all right, but hidden from ourselves as much as from other people. They are not there under wraps: they have not yet been created. We gain access to them, not by somehow going behind behavior, but by letting ourselves go — by behaving more freely. This happens when situations are created in which we are encouraged to be what we are capable of being, situations of trust and mutual appreciation, in which two people draw one another out. When those situations occur, the deeper person we are in search of will be right there in the wistful smiles or imaginative inventions, and will be revealed in what we do as much to ourselves as to anyone else.

That is how two people achieve closeness: when each has the confidence of the other, and each stimulates the other to the inventive things of which we are capable but seldom deliver.

Personal intimacy is thus a rich and unreserved interaction with another person, and therefore even if people's unexpressed thoughts and attitudes were there in their consciousness, and we had some device by means of which we could experience the mental states of other people, personal intimacy would still not prevail. We would not be interacting richly with another person, but rather observing like spectators their conscious processes. Whenever there was any need for the device, that itself would show that there was not intimacy. The way to closeness with and enjoyment of another person is not by coming to know what lies behind the outward shell, but by eliciting from other people the best of which they are capable. For some people and with some people, that is often quite difficult, but it is at least possible; whereas it is neither possible nor what one really wants, to come to know the supposed person behind the smiles and jokes and questions and fits of rage that often seem mere outward show.

An important feature of the picture of personal intimacy we have just sketched is that people appear as sources of creativity that are often dammed up, and that this creativity can be released in some kinds of personal interaction, in which fear and distrust are reduced, self-confidence is generated, and the development and exercise of abilities is stimulated. Creativity here is primarily not a matter of painting pictures, writing books or decorating rooms, but of doing things with another person that are rich and various in their interest and that, unlike party conversation that is designed for universal consumption, expresses the particular interest that two people take in one another.

Hence, to return to our earlier question, "What is good about personal intimacy?" we can now see that wherever it prevails, it releases us from constraints of caution and distrust, which are both thwarting in themselves and tend to make our lives arid. The intimate relationship enriches our lives, both by releasing a creativity of personal interaction that has been inhibited, and by eliciting it from another person.

This, however, still puts it too egocentrically, as if we were talking about an unsuspected way in which another person can be used for maximizing the satisfaction we can get from life. Anyone who approached personal intimacy from this egocentric point of view would not achieve it, because he is not yet so constituted as to find this special kind of relationship good in itself. The slightly paradoxical situation appears to be that the rewards accrue only if one does not aim at them; but this is common to a great many things in life. If we concentrate just on doing something well, the pleasure of so doing it accrues; but if our eye is on the pleasure, our performance will likely be substandard, and whatever enjoyment we derive will not be the satisfaction of a task well performed.

WHY NOT SEX WITHOUT PERSONAL INTIMACY?

So far we have concentrated on explaining the notion of personal intimacy. In doing so it was assumed that this is not an entirely new notion, and that many people care about it, but that it was in need of clarification, both as to what it is and as to what is good about it. Up to this point, except incidentally, we have said nothing as to the bearing of personal intimacy on our sex lives.

In this part of our deliberations it will save a lot of verbiage if we can use expressions like "a purely sexual relationship" or "an impersonal relationship" to mean anything that tends in those directions. Even when sex is put on a commercial basis, it may not always be quite devoid of personal intimacy; and not many of the people who make love casually with near strangers on a Saturday night will be altogether lacking in personal interest in their sex partners. Still, there will not often be much depth of personal interest in such cases, and it would be cumbersome always to construct an expression that allowed for various possible shades and degrees of such interest.

While many people would not want sex without personal intimacy, probably few of those same people, if they had no moral qualms about it, would find sex positively unpleasant just because it lacked personal warmth; and probably many others would not knowingly want and therefore not miss personal intimacy.

It is quite possible to regard sex as essentially a pleasurable activity that happens to require the participation of another person, like dancing. As with dancing, the participants can display skill and style, but it need not matter with whom one is performing, as long as the participants function well together. It would be folly to say that sex, when similarly regarded, need be in any way unrewarding. On the contrary, since it is both a more natural and a more intense pleasure, it is likely to be very much more gratifying than any other activity requiring the participation of someone else.

Yet while sex is not likely to be positively distasteful just through being impersonal, our pleasure in it may be mixed with regrets and dissatisfactions. Whether foolishly or not, many of us are deeply disposed to regard sexual caresses as an expression of affection and enthusiasm for the person who receives them; but when sex is impersonal, caresses come out as an expression of enthusiasm for caressing. If one does not know or care whether the other person is lonely, reads Dickens, likes cats or believes in God, caresses lose their character as expressions of affection. Then there is an emptiness in lovemaking that may be disturbing; and in the case in which one does know and does not like such things about a person, caresses take on the character of falsity.

The disposition to regard sexual tenderness as an expression of affection is not, of course, universal or incurable; but in our culture any other disposition is rare, and it will require either insensitivity or sophistication, when a relationship is primarily sexual, not to wish for personal warmth as well, or to wish one were with someone else with whom there could be such warmth.

From this point of view, when there is personal intimacy between people who make love, they have much the best of it. They want just the person they are with, and have a full relationship with the person they want. There is genuine tenderness in their caresses, which are therefore not only just as pleasant as those of the couple whose lovemaking is mainly sexual, but satisfying to the deep human wish to demonstrate interest and affection.

Hence it may seem much to be recommended that one adopt a policy of making love only with persons for whom one can wholeheartedly express tenderness. Yet while we might admire and commend the sensitivity and concern about personal relationships of anyone who so resolved, it is not clear whether anything else would be foolish, or would show a regrettable want of sensitivity or of concern about personal relationships. It might be that this is the analogue of what in moral contexts is sometimes called supererogatory conduct: acts of conspicuous heroism or extreme generosity, for example. Although these are altogether admirable, failure to perform them is not regarded as a defect.

Not everyone has any talent or taste for close personal relationships, and those who do will not always find others to share themselves with in an intimate way. Our cultural climate tends to make us so cautious, hurried, and pragmatic that close friendships do not develop easily. Hence, although we are passionate fairly constantly, we are on close terms with a suitable person only sometimes; and this can make it seem the better part of wisdom to make love as and when we can, and hope that we will be so fortunate as sometimes to fall into a relationship in which there is also the joy of personal intimacy.

People differ so much, not only in how passionate they are, but in how much they want close friendships and in their aptitude for them, that the answer to the question what is best here will be different from person to person. If one has no interest in personal intimacy there will be no problem, except possibly the question whether one might be turning a blind eye on one of life's joys.

If one does care about the quality of personal relationships, and also requires personal intimacy in one's sex life, then for all but the most outgoing and attractive people, the result will almost certainly be some reduction in the amount of sexual activity one enjoys. However, one may be compensated by the assurance that one's sex life will be rich in the qualities of joy, affection and respect attendant on people's rejoicing in one another as persons.

People who demand personal intimacy in their sex lives may find that having this kind of ideal makes them too self-conscious. They may always be asking themselves, "Is this it? Will my principles permit this?" Not only could these questions be hard to answer with any assurance, the very concern about them could strain the free development of a good relationship. Moreover, the cherished expectation that making love would be particularly splendid might interfere with its spontaneity and cause disappointment.

While not many people would be so deliberate as to encounter this sort of difficulty, perhaps the only general remedy would be the evolution of a cultural climate in which most couples would not make love unless they were on quite special terms, but in which this would not be an ideal that they would list as one of their convictions, or something that was urged upon them by parents and school teachers, but rather something that simply did not happen amongst people who had lived in that climate for any length of time. The thought of making love would perhaps occur to people only when there was an especially warm relationship, or if it occurred to them at other times, it would strike them as a strange or unpleasant idea. Such a cultural climate is not likely to exist soon, but it is perhaps not impossible. Short of that, it is perhaps possible for a person to adopt this attitude deliberately, but over a period of time to make it so much part of the way he functions that it is no longer a principle to which he strives to conform, but instead has become an instinct.

The hardest question is as to the workability of the plan according to which one makes love as fancy dictates or opportunity allows, and hopes that sometimes it will be with someone about whom one cares personally. Clearly this way one might have the best of both worlds: all the sexual satisfaction one wants or fortune provides, some of it under conditions one regards as ideal.

The question as to its workability is whether we can successfully make the switch from one perception of sexual activity to the other; for example, from regarding caresses as a pleasure requiring the participation of another person, to seeing them as an expression of affection and mutual delight. The significance that we can attach to sexual activity, which we discussed in Chapter 1, is a magic and a fragile thing. It is easy to sustain its reality when it is the only way we perceive sexual intimacies, but the danger is that if we sometimes make love when there is no affection or personal delight being expressed, then even when we are with someone for whom we care, the spell may be broken and our intimacies may remain private pleasures happening to require the co-operation of another person. In that case we will have tried to have the best of both worlds and lost. What we lose is something magic and intangible, which not everyone will miss; and since sex will surely still remain extremely pleasant, it is not a loss which leaves us destitute; but still something splendid will have gone from our lives.

Since it is not a moral issue how we handle these matters, it is acceptable that we should all decide for ourselves about them. We differ widely, both in how much we care about what is at stake, and probably also in how readily we can switch back and forth from one perception of sexual activity to another. If we do not care very much about personal intimacy we will perhaps find the risk in trying to have it both ways well worth taking, while if we care intensely even a slight risk may well seem too great.

What we have called personal intimacy is a dimension of human relations to which many people attach importance, and of whose value many others might be persuaded. It is partly out of concern about personal intimacy that many people deplore sexual promiscuity, and many parents worry about whether their children, in their eagerness to experiment with sex, might not be very particular as to whether there is a good personal relationship between them and their sexual partners, and therefore whether they may grow up insensitive to the possibility and the value of personal intimacy.

What has been suggested is that personal intimacy is indeed an excellent thing, deserving of concern and much to be cherished and promoted, but that we make a mistake if we treat it as a matter of moral concern — except in a way that will be indicated shortly. Personal intimacy is therefore not something on which we have a right to insist. It may be regrettable but it is not sinful to relate to people in a generally impersonal way; and it may be excellent but it is not saintly to be caring, interested in and responsive to people in the way described. Possibly people of the latter disposition are more likely also to be morally virtuous, but their moral virtue is a distinct attribute; and it is both possible and common for people of the other disposition to be as honest, generous, fair and courageous as one could wish.

It is no doubt immoral to do anything likely to destroy or adversely affect a good personal relationship, and morally commendable to further and create such relationships. In this one respect, personal intimacy *is* a matter of moral concern; but it is similarly a matter of moral concern whether what I do adversely affects a person's ability to play the violin, although having that ability is not itself a moral virtue.

FOUR

What Are the Ethics of Birth Control, Abortion and Homosexuality?

BIRTH CONTROL

While many people see it as a moral question whether or when or with whom to make love, it would not soon occur to most of us that there was anything morally problematic about whether, if one does make love, to practise birth control. On the face of it, it is as clear as anything could be, that unless the lovers want and will be able to care for a child, it is immoral *not* to use a contraceptive. This varies independently of the morality of the lovemaking itself: if it is immoral that a particular couple should fail to use a contraceptive; and if it is morally acceptable that they should be making love (for example, to take the least controversial case, if they are married), it becomes morally unacceptable if it is undesirable that they should have a child but they take no effective steps to prevent this.

We can imagine special cases in which there could be a moral problem about birth control. If a husband wants children and his wife does not, or vice versa, there might be a problem whether it is immoral for one of them to insist on using contraceptives. Or again if so many people became averse to having children that there was a threat of the extinction of the species, birth control might be controversial. But in the average case in which two people do not want a child, and in which there is no reason why they should and perhaps good reason why they should not, it would seem gratuitous to wonder if it would be immoral of them to use a contraceptive. One could as soon wonder if it was wrong to have a malaria injection before visiting the Panamanian jungle.

Nevertheless, there are people who claim that contraception is immoral, and their claim is worth discussing, not only for the benefit of anyone who does not know whether to take it seriously, but because it leads us into some questions about ourselves that are not only interesting but capable of having important consequences.

Two main arguments are sometimes offered to show that contraception is immoral, only the second of which is of very much interest. The first is that it is wrong because it introduces something unnatural or artificial into human life. That, surprisingly, is the argument *in toto,* and it leaves one baffled as to how the conclusion is supposed to follow. It cannot be denied that contraception does introduce something artificial; but the question is, what is wrong with that? Except in special cases, it is not deceitful, cruel, harmful, unfair, selfish or cowardly; and so unless unnaturalness itself belongs on that list, we need help in seeing what is immoral about it.

There are some unnatural things that are undoubtedly wrong, such as the old Chinese practice of binding girls' feet so that they do not grow, or the practice of making a population docile by introducing tranquilizing chemicals into the water supply; but it is not the unnaturalness of these things that makes them wrong, but their harmfulness or their failure to respect people's right to self-determination. Hence to show in this way that the use of contraceptives is wrong, one would have to show them to be (for example) harmful. Some of them no doubt are harmful, and that is a perfectly good objection to their use; but opponents of birth control are not just opposed to harmful contraceptives, and would consider their argument weakened by any stress on the harmfulness of some of them.

To make the argument work, therefore, it would have to be claimed that the list of properties that make actions wrong includes not only deceitfulness, unfairness, cruelty and cowardice, but also unnaturalness. In other words, we would have to believe that its being unnatural is as basic a reason for thinking an action wrong as that it is cruel or unfair.

That would come as a surprise to people who much as they like what is natural — the countryside, the lambs in spring, the artlessness of children — have not been inclined to think that a thing is defective just because it is unnatural. To ride a bicycle rather than walk, to take medicines when ill, to have an electronic heart-pacer, or to refrain from sexual activity because of moral qualms are all unnatural, perhaps in different senses. Sometimes it is wrong to do these things — if it is someone else's bicycle, for example, or if there are not enough heart-pacers to go around — but it is never wrong just because it is unnatural, not even according to the defenders of the argument we are now considering. The argument, therefore, lacks all force and can be ignored.

The second argument is that the use of contraceptives, whether or not it is unnatural in the sense of artificial, puts us in a position to do something that is unnatural in a different sense: to make love, not for the sake of procreation, which according to this argument is its natural function, but just for the joy of it. Here the objection is not that we use something artificial, even if we do, but that whether we do or not, we are doing something for reasons other than in order to achieve its "natural function."

We have so far only the outline of an argument, the details of which have been filled in by its defenders in various ways. The main problem in fleshing it out is how to have the argument plausibly support the conclusion that the use of contraceptives is immoral, without also entailing such other conclusions as that making love when one or both of the lovers is infertile is morally unacceptable.

The greatest source of difficulties lies in defining a "natural function." One might expect those theologians who propound the argument to say that the natural function of anything is the function God designed it to serve. Such a definition, however, both tends to ensure that the argument will be effective at most among religious believers, and raises problems as to how anyone knows God's intentions. A way of avoiding those awkwardnesses is to say that the natural function of anything is the most important of the possibly desirable consequences it may sometimes have. Here we would talk of the *most important* of the consequences because pregnancy and enjoyment are both consequences of making love, and the latter needs to be excluded. We specify the consequences *it may sometimes have* because pregnancy is not an invariable consequence, but the argument requires that pregnancy be the natural function even when it does not in fact occur. We say the *possibly desirable consequences* (a) because by no means all pregnancies are desirable, while (b) a thing's function could hardly be something that no one ever wants.

The definition of natural function we have devised here nicely avoids some of the difficulties that threaten, but a serious awkwardness remains: it would now appear to follow that it would be wrong to make love except with a view to achieving pregnancy, and hence except on the small number of occasions when pregnancy was desired, total abstinence would be required of us.

It is perhaps possible to accept these implications, but they are extremely restrictive, and not many of the people who defend this kind of argument in fact accept them.

These difficulties might be avoided by giving a different sense to the concept of a natural function. If proponents of the argument said that the natural function of an activity was the most important of the sometimes desirable effects it might have on the actual occasion on which it occurs, then since begetting children is not possible for infertile couples, it would not be the natural function of their sexual activity and they would not be going against that function; and similarly the couple using the rhythm method would (with luck) be making love at times when conception was not possible and was therefore not the natural function of their activity.

Even so, there are some awkward consequences. One of them is that a couple who, not knowing that one of them was infertile, or not knowing anything about the fertile times of the menstrual cycle, took the precaution of using a contraceptive when in fact pregnancy could not have resulted anyway would not be thwarting the natural function of their lovemaking, and would not be doing anything wrong.

Similarly it seems to follow that when a fertile couple uses a contraceptive during a fertile part of the menstrual cycle, then if the contraceptive is an effective one, pregnancy is again not biologically possible, conception is therefore not the "natural function" of the activity, and this couple is doing nothing wrong.

Here we are in the paradoxical position of criticizing an argument for some of its implications, when in fact to most people these implications are perfectly acceptable. The point of course is that the implications contradict the thesis the argument is defending. It is curious that the rhythm method of birth control, which enjoys the approval of many natural function theorists, would come out as immoral, since it leaves conception quite possible, while endeavoring to prevent it.

It may look like a remedy for these difficulties to say in the first case that the couple at least think they are thwarting the natural function of what they are doing, even if they are not in fact, and that is what is wrong; and to say in the second case that the natural function is what would result if the precautions were not taken.

Here it is even more obvious that distinctions are being concocted just to make the argument work; and not surprisingly further difficulties are generated, especially in the second case, where the redefinition of the natural function as what would result if precautions were not taken revives all the difficulties from which we were saved by restricting the application of the argument to cases in which pregnancy could in fact occur.

We would be backsliding in a similar way if we were to say that the special feature that makes the use of a contraceptive a thwarting of the natural function, when the rhythm method is not, is that the former introduces something artificial into human life; but we have already seen the bankruptcy of general objections to what is artificial.

We can see from the foregoing how very unclear is the notion of a natural function. The fundamental obscurity of the idea makes possible a multitude of shifts and twists in the argument, some of the most typical of which have been displayed here; but it also has the consequence that any argument developed will be a very fragile thing, shored up with distinctions introduced for no better reason than to make the argument yield the desired conclusion, without at the same time having implications that are not desired.

A further illustration of how confused this idea of natural functions is lies in the fact that, while enjoyment and fatigue are much more regular consequences of sexual activity than pregnancy, and occur as naturally as one could require, they are never listed as natural functions. An obvious reason for this is that one could not in that way construct an argument against the use of contraceptives; but that makes the choice of begetting children as the natural function seem somewhat arbitrary.

We have so far been considering the internal workings of these arguments, and have not asked whether any of the shifting principles on which they rely are points of morals to which we must assent. For example, is it recognized as morally defective to do something for reasons other than in order to bring about the natural consequence of so acting?

If a principle is a recognized point of morals, it will be surprising if there are not ready to hand some clear and familiar applications of it; but in this case it is peculiarly difficult to find anything that is both a clear application of the principle, and clearly morally defective. It is scarcely believable that it is immoral to sail a boat to yonder point, not particularly wanting to get there, but only to have a pleasant sail, nor is it obviously wrong to continue working only because you enjoy working when you already have as much money as you want. It is not of course perfectly clear whether either of these is an application of the principle, but that itself helps show what an obscure principle it is.

To help someone, not out of concern for his welfare, but to create a good impression, or to be friendly, not out of affection but to curry favor, are defective modes of behavior done for reasons other than to achieve their natural upshot. Perhaps cases like these lend the principle any plausibility it has; still it is the deviousness of these actions, not their being in some obscure way unnatural, that makes them wrong; and there is nothing devious about making love but taking steps to see that the natural consequences do not ensue.

Perhaps the fact that all through history there have been thinkers who have been attracted by the project of basing moral conclusions on some concept of the natural shows, even if the project has never succeeded, that there is something important here waiting to be brought out. Yet even if it came to be undeniable that it is a moral imperfection to use a contraceptive, one could not responsibly press for the absolute avoidance of this sin, knowing that the certain result would be an increase in the incidence of unwanted pregnancies. It is not yet clear that avoiding the unnatural is excellent at all, but if it is a good thing it is hardly so very good as to outweigh anything so undesirable as an unwanted pregnancy. Not that there is no third possibility—there is always sexual abstinence—but that is at best likely to be adopted in no more than a very small number of cases.

A quite different form of argument against contraception is sometimes heard: if life is a good thing, it is surely good to have as many people partaking of it as possible, and we should not do anything to restrict the number. By this reasoning, every woman should produce children unremittingly during all the years she is capable of it, yet this consequence is not acceptable even to defenders of the argument. If the argument were qualified by providing that the duty to multiply is upon us only where and so long as life is good, it would entail that a prosperous couple in a region not overpopulated should have as many children as the woman's fertile years will allow, but even that limited conclusion is not acceptable to anyone who recognizes the clear advantages to all concerned of restricting the size of families.

It is not even clear whether the above qualification is defensible.

Things would have to be very grim indeed before many people would be found who preferred not to live, and therefore until overpopulation reached a point where large numbers of people stopped having this preference, it would be true that life is a good thing, and it would follow as much or as little as it ever did that there should be as many people to partake of it as possible.

The question is, does this follow? If it did, we would have to say that there is at least a consideration there. It may have to be weighed against other considerations, and may very often come out second best, but at least in some cases it would prevail.

The reasoning here is similar to that in the sound argument, "If health is good, the more people who are healthy, the better," and derives its plausibility from this likeness; but there are important differences. The health argument shows only that the more of the *existing* people who are healthy, the better, and does not show that we should produce more people, any more than if a film is delightful we should enlarge the human race so that more people can enjoy it. One can exist but not be healthy, or exist but not see a certain film, but one cannot exist and not have life. We can increase the number of existing people who see a film or are healthy, but we cannot increase the number of existing people who have life.

We can fail to provide someone with health, education or pleasure and it can be morally remiss of us, but we cannot fail to provide someone with life, because there is not yet anyone to whom that advantage is denied. If there were souls not yet supplied with bodies waiting for entry into this world, and those waiting existed in disagreeable conditions, we might have a quite serious duty to procreate. But it is not clear whether what we have just supposed makes any sense; and even if it does, our reasons for believing it are too slight by far to make it a consideration deserving to be weighed against things that we have very good reasons to believe.

It might be argued that there is a duty to procreate of a very special and wonderful sort. Whereas most duties are *to* someone—

there is someone on whom we confer a benefit, and if we fail in our duty someone is deprived of a benefit — in this case both beneficiary and benefit are the fruit of one and the same act.

If a couple living on a lovely island think: "Children would love it here. Let's have some!", they are not necessarily thinking of how much they would enjoy the children's delight. They may embark on parenthood primarily for the benefit of the (as yet non-existing) children. This seems to show that it is possible to do something for someone who does not exist. But this is an act of generosity, rather than a duty. It is not something that could be required of people; and it is absurd to suppose that people could be made generous in this very special way, either by being bound to procreate or by being forbidden to use contraceptives.

Moreover, it is a different story if our couple lives, not on a lovely island, but in circumstances in which the most they could think is: "Children living here would prefer living to not living. Let's have some!" The procreative activity has now lost its character as an act of generosity, and cannot even be admired, still less enjoined.

It is probably fair to say that the foregoing are the three main types of argument that are advanced against the use of contraceptives. There are many versions of these arguments, and it is difficult to be sure that one has fairly stated the strongest versions, or that one has come to terms with the essentials of this or that type of argument; but if the arguments we have discussed are representative, it is clear that no argument against birth control can command any serious respect.

When intelligent people persistently advance transparently weak arguments, and nimbly shift from one to another, there is reason to suspect some motivation lying behind the endeavor that its authors are shy of professing. Such motivations can be either reputable or otherwise. Let us not discuss the latter. There is a kind of argument for which one might have some respect, although it is never in fact used, and it could be put this way:

Indiscriminate sexual activity is wrong for all kinds of reasons, but these reasons are hard to explain and to impress upon people in the mass. Some people will understand and be impressed, but that is not enough. It is important that everyone should exercise sexual restraint. There is, however, one consideration that functions for almost anyone as a strong deterrent to sexual activity, namely the danger of pregnancy. If that danger is removed, as it will be by the use of contraceptives, indiscriminate sexual activity will still be wrong but very many more people will engage in it. Hence, if people could be persuaded not to use contraceptives, the deterrent value of the danger of pregnancy would remain operative, and the sex lives of very many more people would be in conformity with sound morality.

This line of thinking expresses a serious concern, and recognizes the important fact that, for good or ill, people will make love much more freely if effective contraceptives are readily available to them. Nevertheless, some serious objections can be made:

1. If the argument leads to saying that the use of contraceptives is wrong, then it is a disingenuous argument. It is not the use of contraceptives but the indiscriminate sexual activity that is supposed to be wrong.

2. The machinery proposed is too crude and unselective in its application: it tends to restrict sexual activity whether indiscriminate or not. The lovemaking of a married couple is as much interfered with as that of the sexual adventurer.

3. It is irresponsible in its disregard for the question of the incidence of unwanted pregnancies. If contraceptives were either unavailable or not used by many people as being immoral, then while the sexual activity of some people would be curtailed, others would proceed as before but without precaution, and there would be more ill-advised marriages, disrupted careers, and children for whose care there was no adequate provision.

4. If indiscriminate sexual activity is wrong for reasons other than the risk of pregnancy, the reasons for its wrongness cannot be so very abstruse and hard to explain; and it would seem the better

part of wisdom to state and reiterate those reasons clearly, rather than ask people to believe the least believable moral proposition imaginable, namely that it is wrong to take effective and harmless steps to reduce the incidence of an undesirable phenomenon.

ABORTION

The question of the morality of abortion is one that any sexually active woman, and with her any man who has had a part in the pregnancy that gives rise to the question of abortion, is likely to face at some time or other. It is one of the most perplexing of moral questions. One can, it is true, take a strong stand on one side or other of the issue, and assemble plausible arguments in its support; but on neither side of the issue do the arguments ever come close to settling the question.

In many cases, there are sound reasons why, other things being equal or ignored, an abortion would be morally desirable. There may already be so many children in a family that the parents are not able to provide adequately for them, and are going out of their minds with the confusion and strain; or a pregnant girl may be quite unequipped for the responsibilities of motherhood, so that her child will be doomed either to a life of poverty with its mother, or a dismal life in orphanages and foster homes; or a woman may have been raped by someone whose child she neither wants nor deserves to bear and rear; and so forth.

In some of these cases, other people are making a choice, on behalf of a prospective human being, between a life that is grim and no life at all. Most people if they had that choice to make themselves would choose to live; and most of us would be appalled at the thought of taking it upon ourselves to make the choice on behalf of someone who was ten, twenty or thirty years old. The thought of putting a person to death because he is having a rough time of it and might be better dead cannot seriously be entertained; and yet it is not an entirely different thought from that of destroying a fetus because it will likely have a difficult life.

Moreover, some considerations of the type we mentioned are more weighty than others. Considerations of convenience to the parents, while they may in some cases deserve to be taken seriously, will in general seem too slight to be weighed against the life of a human being. When an undesirable prospect is something no person can counteract, such as the likelihood of serious deformity, that is a more telling consideration than a prospect that can be avoided by efforts of varying degrees of strenuousness on the part of the parents or of other persons. If it is only because in a given society unwanted children are shabbily provided for that the prospects for such a child are grim, it seems fair to say, "Better to improve those arrangements than to dispose of the child"; and similarly if it will only be difficult to provide for the child, but it could be done, it seems fair to say, "Better to make the effort than to dispose of the child." But even if in these ways the considerations favoring abortion vary in weight, they do in very many cases have considerable weight, and cannot be set aside as not deserving to be taken seriously at all.

In the above reflections, it was repeatedly assumed that having an abortion is taking the life of a human being, and it is this of course that generates the problem. There is nothing problematic about whether to do something that will lessen human suffering, as long as the price of doing so is not some detriment to someone else. If having an abortion were like having a cyst removed, or like deciding before conception not to have a child, there would either be no problem at all or not the special kind of problem that abortion generates. The prime moral argument against abortion is that it takes a human life; that abortion is tantamount to murder, and therefore morally wrong if anything is.

If it were perfectly clear that abortion is a form of murder, or is tantamount to murder, there would be very little room for discussion of whether the practice is morally defensible. Some morally important things can be weighed in the balance against other things and come out second best, but perhaps the only thing that can be weighed against a human life is another human life; and if so, and if to have an abortion is to take a life, the only case of abortion that would be seriously discussable would be that in which the life of a mother was weighed against that of her child. Such cases do arise, and are difficult, but since few of the cases in which anyone wants an abortion are so extreme, our discussion will be confined to the more everyday cases.

An argument that having an abortion is not taking a human life, and not tantamount to murder, might run somewhat as follows. Murder is the intentional killing of a human being, and to be human anything must resemble normal members of our species both physically and psychologically. But a fetus, or at least an embryo, does not resemble a human being. It does not have arms, legs, or a face. It does not experience pleasure or pain, does not hope or fear, and neither loves nor is loved. Killing it therefore is not killing a human being and is not murder.

The point here might be illustrated vividly this way. One person plots to kill his enemy. The intended victim hides and is found, runs and is caught, struggles and is overcome, is stabbed and feels fear and pain, and dies in the arms of his grieving mother. Another person administers an injection or performs a simple surgical procedure, and soon a small wiggling thing in a woman's womb ceases to wiggle. The wiggling thing was not this person's enemy and was not pursued relentlessly. It did not want life, fear death, struggle or suffer pain; and no one grieved over its loss, remembering good times together and wondering how life could continue without it.

Can the actions of these two persons be the same morally? There is a much greater difference between them than there is between one murder and another: between the killing of an enemy and wanton killing; between killing someone who will be missed and someone who will not. The embryo is not only not an enemy, it is not possible that it should be; and similarly it is not possible for it to be afraid or feel pain, and not possible to reminisce about it or miss its company.

It is not true, however, contrary to what some people maintain, that the elimination of a fetus is an act of just the same kind as the removal of a wart or a tumor. The hard fact about a fetus is that although it is not yet a human being, it is something that would, in the normal course of events, become one. Whether this fact makes a moral difference is not settled by recognizing it as a fact; but neither may the moral question be settled by denying this fact.

When this point in thinking about abortion is reached, an approach that has suggested itself to many people is that of laying down the principle that abortion becomes wrong at the point at which a fetus becomes a human being, and then addressing oneself to the question, what point is that?

In posing the problem this way, one must assume that abortion is not wrong prior to the point, whatever it is, at which a fetus becomes a human being—and it is not yet perfectly clear whether we are entitled to assume this. Quite apart from that difficulty, however, it is almost certainly a dead end to press the question when a fetus becomes human. One can choose and stick by an answer to that question, but there will be something arbitrary about any answer chosen. Taking the most promising argument, that a fetus is a human being when it reaches the stage of development at which it can survive outside the womb, there are at least two difficulties: (i) new methods of caring for prematurely born infants in the past fifty years have probably pushed the date at which an infant can survive outside the womb back about a month, but it seems absurd to say that a fetus of six and a half months is a human being today, but would not have been fifty years ago; (ii) there is not likely to be much difference between a fetus just before and just after it becomes capable of surviving outside the womb. Perhaps some valve becomes operational, or two bits of nervous tissue grow together allowing the breathing mechanism to function but can we really suppose that such a small difference makes such a large difference?

A somewhat similar question may be posed by some people who are religious. They may see it as a question of when the soul joins the body, on the supposition that it is immoral to kill anything that has a soul, but not otherwise. This is as much a dead end as the other. Not only will there be no way of deciding when the soul arrives; it will not be clear why that should make a moral difference. Is it perhaps that one is tampering, not just with the earthly economy, but with the heavenly one, by forcing a soul to retire and await another opportunity to have a body, or perhaps even by depriving a soul of its one chance to have a body?

There is a general objection to any attempt to decide when a fetus becomes a human being: even if the question were decidable, the fetus prior to passing that point is still something that will in the normal course of events become a human being. It will be true of the thing in the womb at whatever stage in its development we take it, that it is on the way to being human. It is true from the moment of conception that there is something there that, unlike a cyst, will in the course of time be a person. A human fetus, however unlike a mature human being it may be at some stages of its development, is from the beginning recognizably a human fetus.

We have not yet discussed, however, whether the clear difference that exists between a fetus, even at its earliest stages, and a wart or a tumor, does indeed make the killing of a fetus morally objectionable. We might approach that question this way:

If cutting down oak trees were a crime, it would not, just on that account, be a crime to gather acorns, or even to destroy oak sprouts, although acorns and oak sprouts are potential oak trees. One could make these things a crime also; and one's decision would depend on such things as whether one wanted to have as many oak trees in the world as possible, whether it was the current value of oak trees, for their shade or their beauty or all that had gone into growing them over the years, that was the basis of the rule against cutting them down, or perhaps whether the oak was a national or a religious symbol, so that any disrespect for it was a traitorous or a sacrilegious act. In the first and the third of these cases, but not in the second, we would have a reason for making harm to acorns and oak sprouts a crime.

Can we suggest and evaluate reasons we might similarly offer, given that killing human beings is a crime, for making it a crime also to kill potential human beings? Just as the destruction of acorns is not the same thing as the destruction of oak trees, so destroying a fetus is not the same as killing a grown person; just as it would not follow from the fact that cutting down oaks was a crime, that gathering acorns was, so it does not follow from the fact that killing people is wrong, that destroying a fetus is; but also just as there might be further considerations that would lead us also to prohibit gathering acorns, there may be reasons why we should also prohibit the destruction of a fetus.

It is easy to see that it is not the desirability of there being as many people as possible that would lead us to prohibit abortions: there are too many people as it is. Special groups of people might discourage abortions for this sort of reason: a church, with a view to having as many adherents as possible, or a country that was underpopulated or fearful of being overrun, or had ambitions to overrun other countries; but these would not be considerations making it wrong for people other than members of that church or citizens of that country to have an abortion.

Some political radicals may find the increase in population resulting from the prohibition of abortion desirable, in that it will worsen the appalling conditions of life in poor countries, and so hasten the revolution. This, however, is not an argument that the generality of citizens of such countries could take seriously.

If abortion were wrong because of the need for more people, then not only would it be wrong only when there was a need for more people, but it would not be clear that even then it was wrong in each and every case. The couple who already had ten children, for example, could be deemed to have made a fair contribution and be exempted from the prohibition.

Moreover, on these conditions not taking steps to conceive would be as much a crime as having an abortion, women would be under a duty to be pregnant at all times, and men to see to it that they were.

Continuing to apply the pattern of investigation from our oak tree case, if it is the current value of a human being that makes it wrong to kill, then abortion will either not be wrong or will be a very minor crime, because an unborn child has little current value, and none of the *kind* of current value that a mature human being has. However, it is not the current value of human beings that makes it wrong to kill them. It is a very basic part of our moral thinking that people's lives must be respected regardless of their current value, and regardless of the effort that has gone into making them what they are. The right to life of the idiot and the thief is as much respected as that of the genius and the saint. It is as wrong to kill a young person as a mature one, and to kill someone with no education as someone expensively educated.

We have now considered an argument for and an argument against prohibiting the killing of potential human beings as well as actual ones, and found both of them to fail. We should not take our acorn/oak tree model as necessarily canvassing all the possibilities, but on that model there remains a third kind of argument to be considered. Whether or not it is in itself a bad thing to destroy a fetus, respect for potential persons is an integral part of something very important, namely respect for human life. Respect for life will be weakened if we allow ourselves to become indifferent to near-human life, as represented in the fetus. Hence, in order to keep the former intact and strong, we must not allow the latter to set in. We do not want it to come about that it does not seem a bad thing to kill someone who is weak or unimportant, or to kill someone when it can be done impersonally, without seeing the fear or the pain. When an abortion is performed, something is killed that is weak and thought to be unimportant. It is done clinically, without confronting the thing killed or seeing it die. A person who could not face strangling a newborn infant will, a few months earlier, bring about the same result with scarcely a qualm.

Two things in this line of thinking are quite unclear:

1. It is not clear whether its conclusion is that although abortion is not always morally wrong, there are good reasons of social

policy for treating it as being morally wrong, namely that if people become morally indifferent to abortion, they are more likely to become morally indifferent to the killing of the old, the deformed, the mentally ill and the weak, and to the killing of anyone when it can be done impersonally; for example, by planting bombs in letter boxes or dropping them from planes.

2. It is not clear what kind of connection is supposed to exist between moral indifference to abortion and moral indifference to these other things. Is it that although there are differences between abortion and these other things, such that one of them can be right while the others are wrong, not everyone will perceive the differences, and those that do not might conclude that if abortion is acceptable, these other things must be too? Or is there supposed to be a logical connection, such that we cannot consistently say that abortion is morally acceptable, but killing the old, the deformed and the weak is not?

Clearly if our decision to represent abortion as wrong were based, not on what we called the logical connection, but on our doubts as to whether everyone would perceive the moral difference between killing fetuses and other kinds of killing, then the answer to the first of the above questions would be that, for reasons of social policy, we are representing abortion as wrong irrespective of its wrongness.

Let us first ask whether there might be good reasons for taking such a stand. There are at least three considerations that render this doubtful.

1. Its soundness would appear to depend quite heavily on the prevalence of a cultural climate in which little attempt is made to bring it about that many people understand the morals of the community. If we rely heavily on merely prohibiting certain kinds of action, without teaching people to think for themselves and make distinctions between cases, then whenever there are two actions superficially resembling one another, we must expect that

many people will go by that superficial resemblance, and take one to be acceptable if the other is. To the extent that a more comprehending approach to the morals of the community is brought about, it will not be necessary to make blanket prohibitions of actions, without regard to whether they are always wrong. However, in the present cultural climate, perhaps such policies are often necessary.

2. The careless and unintelligent people at whom blanket prohibitions are directed are likely to sin when it suits their purposes no matter what the law or the official morality prescribes. Hence moral policies tailored for the less concerned and less intelligent members of the species are likely to be a misdirected and largely wasted effort.

3. When prevailing attitudes are such that a legal prohibition makes little difference to whether an action is thought wrong or to the frequency with which it is performed, the main effect of prohibiting anything which, like abortion, requires the skilled assistance of another person, is to make it more expensive and more dangerous. Prohibitions enrich people who are prepared to traffic illegally in the prohibited commodity or service, and endanger the health and the lives of consumers of those commodities and services.

Let us now consider the question in a more fundamental way — not from the point of view of social policy, but from that of an individual considering whether to have or to recommend an abortion, regardless of what the law or the official morality provides. The question will be either: although not prohibited, is abortion wrong, or although prohibited, is it something a responsible person could have, perform or advise?

The first point to be made is that one cannot, in one's own case, be moved by such thoughts as that if one were to decide that abortion is morally acceptable, one would soon find oneself morally indifferent to the lives of the old, the weak and the deformed, or more inclined to do wrong when it can be done without confronting the person who will suffer. If that argument has any application, it applies not to people who responsibly decide, but to people who unthinkingly inherit an attitude from the community, and who cannot make distinctions between similar but different cases. In the very thinking of the argument, one recognizes and reaffirms the wrongness of the things to which one supposes oneself becoming morally indifferent. In the very project of deciding for oneself, one claims the ability to make distinctions between different cases. Anyone who seriously thought he could not do that could not responsibly embark on the project of making his own decision.

The question therefore is not one of what we will, in spite of ourselves, soon find our attitudes to be if we decide in favor of abortion, but what we called a "logical" question: whether we can consistently hold abortion to be acceptable, while holding it wrong to kill the old, the weak and the deformed.

This question is made peculiarly difficult by the fact that the moral principles that we would want to apply to the case are designed to govern the relations between ordinary functioning human beings, and do not contemplate the case of a near or a potential human being. It is the desire to live, the fear of death, the annihilation of plans and ambitions, the grief of friends, and the right to self-determination that we think of when we ask why it is wrong to kill a functioning human being; but these considerations do not immediately apply to a fetus. A fetus is something that will eventually want to live, fear death, have plans and ambitions, be loved and be able to determine its own destiny, but in its fetal stage none of these considerations is quite applicable. It is, therefore, possible consistently to favor abortion while being opposed to the killing of other human beings resembling the fetus in some of their incapacities: for hope, fear, pain, ambition, love or self-determination. Our ordinary moral principles do not quite reach the case of the fetus. To be morally opposed to abortion is an extension of our principles beyond their normal application, an extension not logically required, but on the other hand not logically repugnant either.

So far, although we have canvassed most of the usual arguments on both sides of the abortion issue, we have not only not found anything that is conclusive for or against it, we have found nothing sufficiently telling even to justify a reasonable preference. The question seems to be beyond the range of application of our ordinary principles, and calls for a decision that cannot be represented as in any way necessitated by any recognized form of reasoning. If this decision is to be made other than quite arbitrarily, perhaps the main questions to be asked in considering it are:

1. Do you regard as important the fact that a fetus will, in the normal course of events, become a human being? In another year or two what is now a collection of cells will be someone full of joy and curiosity, eager for life and fearful of death. Does the fact that it is not now such a being make a difference, and if so, why?

2. Could you bring yourself to suffocate or poison a child once born, and if not, what difference do you see between that and terminating the life of a fetus?

3. If, from the moment of conception, human beings developed, not in the womb, but visibly in incubators, where they were nourished and tended, so that it took either neglect or some positive act to terminate their life, could you bring yourself to perform that act?

It is not suggested that every responsible and humane person must answer these questions in the same way. Perspectives on life are imaginable that command respect and make abortion morally reputable. For example, someone might say something like this: "Life is not intrinsically valuable. Nature is very profligate with it. Not only is all life, including our own, at the mercy of diseases and natural disasters, but one species preys on others without mercy, and some are even given to eating their own young. Except with regard to their own kind, human beings are not, with some exceptions, great respecters of life. We hunt and fish, raise domestic animals for slaughter, and are not always averse to disposing of pets when it becomes inconvenient to keep them. We have seen fit to cultivate some restraints on the natural cheapness of life, but these are essentially practical devices, good only insofar as they enable us to live peaceably together and divert our limited energies from self-protection, which would otherwise occupy too much of our attention, to more rewarding pursuits. We have, however, tended to make a mystique out of the rules against the destruction of human life, representing them, not as practical devices, but as derived from the inherent value of life. It is when so considered that the rules create problems about suicide, euthanasia and abortion. But something has got out of hand here. In our anxiety to impress the rules on each and every person we have exaggerated their solemnity. We should divest them of this solemnity and confine their application to the important but limited functions for which they were conceived."

We might imagine that in the society this person envisages, while people would be every bit as punctilious as we are about human life insofar as any individual wanted to live and stood some chance of finding life rewarding, no one would see any particular problem about the morality of abortion; it would not be a crime to assist in the suicide of someone who seriously and for good reason wanted to die; it would not be the duty of doctors to prolong the lives of people with terminal diseases; and perhaps homicidal maniacs would be put to death, not as a punishment for their crimes, but because no value and much danger was seen in their continuing to live.

It is not suggested that if we treated abortion as morally acceptable, we would be logically required to adopt all of these other attitudes, but only that if we ceased to represent all human life as intrinsically valuable, we would be free to adopt any of them.

If we were to read of a society in which there was this much indifference to life, but in which also there was both scrupulous concern about the preservation of life insofar as there was a prospect of its being rewarding, and respect for each person's desire to live, we could respect that society. It would not be out of the question to go and live among its members, and it would not be clearly urgent that they be converted to something more like our way of thinking. Theirs is one of the directions in which we may be tending if we favor abortion on demand. The question each person must answer is: Do I seriously want to go in that direction, or in one like it?

A final pair of questions that should be raised is: given that we are right in supposing that a decision about the abortion question goes beyond and is not necessitated by recognized moral principles, and given that someone decides against abortion, (a) has that person a right to disapprove of those who favor it, and (b) what stand is it reasonable for him to take on the question of making or keeping it illegal?

These questions are made especially difficult by our supposition that the decision goes beyond recognized moral principles. In the normal case in which one disapproves of something, either it is clearly wrong and the other person knows it to be wrong, but does it anyway, or his believing it not to be wrong represents some fairly clear self-deception on his part. He has perhaps rationalized it to suit his purposes. And in the normal case in which something is criminal, its prohibition is quite clearly vital to the orderly functioning of society. Deceiving one's husband, jilting one's girl friend or cheating at cards, however wrong they may be conceived to be, are not made criminal offences, because they do not interfere sufficiently with the orderly functioning of our lives.

If we are right in supposing that the abortion question takes us beyond recognized principles, anyone's decision that it is nevertheless wrong will not generate the usual conditions for disapproval, that anyone having, performing or advising an abortion either knows it to be wrong but does it anyway, or is self-deceived. Nor will it be clear that the practice of abortion, however wrong it may be thought, is sufficiently detrimental to the orderly conduct of our lives to be considered a criminal act.

This is not to say that there would be no justification in any circumstances for disapproving of abortion, or making it a criminal act. One could perhaps deplore the heedlessness of someone who had performed or advised an abortion with no thought whatever except for human convenience — though it is a hard question whether in that case it is the abortion or the heedlessness that is deplored. What one could not do is disapprove of the person who, having considered the question honestly, has arrived at a different conclusion.

Concerning the question whether there are any conditions under which abortion might be made a criminal act, two suggestions might be offered:

1. If the failure to prohibit something amounts to a social declaration of its moral acceptability, and if there is a serious, though not confidently answerable question as to its moral acceptability, there might appear to be a reason for prohibiting it *just to keep the serious moral question alive.* If it is not prohibited, then large numbers of people will put the question out of their minds and have abortions as casually as they have tonsillectomies.

While this does seem an important consideration, there are three points to be made against it:

(a) There are other ways of keeping moral questions alive. There is no law against many of the lies we tell, or the unkind things we do, but we have managed to keep the conviction fairly well established that deception and unkindness are moral defects.

(b) It is probably only in the transitional period between the time when a prohibition is withdrawn and the time when other ways of discouraging the formerly prohibited act take effect that the absence of an official declaration of moral unacceptability generates moral indifference.

(c) If anything is criminally prohibited, there must be penalties provided. A law without penalties will not be taken seriously, and one with light penalties will not serve as a serious declaration of moral unacceptability. But if a law is kept in force just to keep a moral question alive, and not to restrict an unacceptable interference with the orderly functioning of our lives, it is barbarous to make the penalty a grave one. Anything but a grave penalty, however, will not serve as a declaration of unacceptability, and will not keep the question alive.

2. If criminal prohibitions were withdrawn and it became clear after a time that the availability of abortions was having serious repercussions — if, for example, it was found that there was a marked increase in the incidence of mental disorders, or that people became markedly less humane, and if these conditions could be attributed with some confidence to the increase in the frequency of abortions—there might appear to be a good reason for reinstituting the prohibitions.

This is in fact sometimes offered as a reason: but one must suspect its authors of relying on prognostications, rather than on what has been found to be the case. They would favor the prohibition of abortion whether its legality had these consequences or not. They are like opponents of the legalization of marijuana who argue that we do not know yet what effects it may have on our health. They do not advocate that the sale of cigarettes should be illegal, although they *do* know smoking is bad for our health, and they would be opposed to marijuana whether it was unhealthy or not.

However, if it was not merely feared but known that some very undesirable consequences would ensue, there would be a case for retaining or instituting legal prohibitions. The question would not be settled thereby: we would have to weigh that consideration against others that we have mentioned in other connections, chiefly: (a) whether the practice of abortion could not be discouraged in other ways, such as the ways in which we discourage people from smoking, or drinking too much; and (b) whether the consequences of legal prohibitions — the profiteering, the substandard medical procedures — are not more to be deplored than the consequence of the availability of abortions.

Anyone who regarded abortion as tantamount to murder would of course regard the considerations we have been mentioning in discussing disapproval of or legal prohibition of abortion as too slight to count for anything against the grave wrong that is being done in destroying a fetus. To worry about profiteering, for example, would seem to that person to be on a par with worrying about how the price of hired killers will rise if we make murder a crime. The last part of the discussion has been premised on and only makes sense given our conclusion that a decision as to the morality of abortion goes beyond and is not required by any recognized moral principles. One may indeed go beyond these principles; but to do so and decide that abortion is wrong is not to decide that it is a special case of murder. To regard the decision that way would be to treat the abortion question as being within the purview of a recognized moral principle.

The person who substantially agrees with these arguments and also makes a decision against abortion will of course not have, perform or advise an abortion, may bring up children to regard it as abhorrent, and may grasp every opportunity to persuade adults of this. What that person may not do is: (i) make such claims as that abortion is tantamount to murder; (ii) treat anyone who favors abortion as morally defective; (iii) assume that its wrongness entails without more ado that it should be a criminal offence.

HOMOSEXUALITY

Not very many of us have to face the question of whether to engage in homosexual practices, because not many of us have any interest in doing so; but for anyone who does find that persons of the opposite sex are not sexually interesting and persons of the same sex are, that question will arise; and for all of us the question will arise what attitude to adopt towards anyone who is homosexual.

In our culture, it is likely to be, in varying degrees, imprudent to pursue a homosexual course in life. It is unlikely to remain secret for very long; and anyone who is believed to be homosexual may be avoided, ridiculed, jeered at, dismissed from employment, blackmailed. Some fortunate homosexuals manage to carve out an acceptable life for themselves notwithstanding society's intolerance, but this is achieved with some difficulty, and no one is likely to avoid painful incidents entirely. Hostility to homosexuals is not universal, but it is sufficiently widespread to make the life of a person who is homosexual range from being somewhat difficult to being indescribably miserable; and this makes it imprudent, if one has any choice in the matter, to become a practising homosexual, and immoral — if it can be done — to convert a person to homosexuality.

It is not perfectly clear whether by persuading someone to join with you in homosexual activity that person can in fact, if not previously much interested in persons of the same sex, be converted to homosexuality. Just as we can be sexually stimulated in masturbation and by various artificial devices, so a person might find it convenient to enlist others of the same sex in stimulating and relieving sexual passion without finding those persons sexually attractive—without, if it is a man, coming to look on some men with that peculiar excitement and tenderness with which a heterosexual male looks on some women. If that is a test of whether one is homosexual, it does seem possible to engage in homosexual practices without being homosexual. Be that as it may, if it is true that the life of a homosexual is generally unhappy, then *if* a person can be converted to homosexuality, the act of conversion is immoral.

That is not to say, however, that being homosexual is itself immoral. If it is a difficult and unhappy course of life, it is certainly imprudent, but is it also immoral? By the test of immorality we have been using, it would not appear so. While homosexual relations, like any other, *can* be deceitful, cruel, harmful, unfair, cowardly or selfish, they need not be and are not generally defective in any of these ways; and where one or other of these moral defects appears, it is not the homosexuality that is wrong, but only the deceit or the cruelty.

In reply to this someone may say that deceit, cruelty and the rest are not the only kinds of immorality; there is also unnaturalness. Homosexual practices are unnatural in that they engage sexuality for purposes other than its natural function of procreation and hence are immoral.

It is not clear, however, as we saw in discussing birth control, that whatever is unnatural is immoral. Heterosexual activity between persons who wish to avoid procreation is unnatural in exactly the same sense of employing one's sexuality for purposes other than procreation; and the average opponent of homosexuality will not also say that the couple with six children who still make love, using a contraceptive, are acting immorally. Nor is it immoral to eat when not hungry, to use the heel of a shoe to drive a nail or to write a letter holding the pen in your mouth, although in all these cases something is being used for other than its natural function.

If homosexual activity is not, at least when carried through without cruelty, unfairness, deception or other moral defect, immoral, is there any other way in which it is defective?

Homosexual and heterosexual relationships are alike in being capable of being personal or impersonal. Just as one may hire someone of the opposite sex for a sexual engagement, so one may hire someone of the same sex; just as one may get together sexually with someone of the opposite sex in whom one has no personal interest, so may one with someone of the same sex; and just as a man and a woman may find one another mutually entertaining in a large number of ways including sexually, and still not care for one another, so may two men or two women. But homosexual relations can also be as deep and as personal as can heterosexual relations.

There are factors that make it difficult for a homosexual friendship to be intimate: the fact, for example, that it will tend to be haunted somewhat by the spectre of public distaste; or that it cannot often be reinforced by or rounded out by the cheerful acceptance by family and friends; and that persons who are homosexual are often less stable emotionally than the average man or woman. But these things only make deep personal relationships somewhat more difficult: many people who are homosexual are more genuine in their feeling for people than many who are not. Indeed, the latter, not being tested in the fires of public scorn and derision, may often end up as the shallower persons.

One does not, however, often hear such high-minded objections to homosexuality as we have been discussing. The kind of objection that is much more likely to be voiced is that what homosexuals *do* together is so distasteful. How could we respect someone, or associate with someone, who does those things?

All sexual behavior can seem astonishing, looked at from the point of view of our standard public demeanor on a bus, at the office or on the tennis court, where for all the world you would think that human beings were interested only in such things as weather, work, sports, music and astronomy. You would hardly guess that there was this strange undercurrent of our lives. If a nonsexual being from another planet came and lived among us for a while, learning our games, discussing our science, reading our newspaper editorials and going to our concerts, he might well be surprised and disgusted when it dawned on him that as well as doing all these things, we retire to secluded spots, strip off all our clothes and in a strange frenzy apply ourselves to one another the way we do — but he would find the homosexual version of this frenzy no more surprising than the heterosexual.

Some of the ways in which people of opposite sexes engage with one another sexually can seem disgusting to people whose approach to these matters is more restrained; but not many of the people who are disgusted by homosexuality enquire how a heterosexual couple goes about making love, or despise people known to be innovative in their heterosexual practices. If they are of opposite sexes, it is all right whatever it is. This suggests that it is not what homosexuals do that is found disgusting, it is just that whatever it is, it is between persons of the same sex.

Hearty heterosexuals will, of course, not usually have any taste for homosexual practices; but just as, if I find oysters disagreeable and say they disgust me, I ought not to go on to say that it is disgusting that anyone should enjoy them, or that I would not care to have anything to do with a person who did, so I should not, if I would find a man's caresses unpleasant, say it is disgusting that any man should enjoy them.

We may take this leap from our own distaste to the objective distastefulness if we are ourselves sexually insecure; if we are not quite certain what our sexual tastes are or if we fear even to be suspected of homosexuality by someone else. We proclaim our stout heterosexuality — to ourselves and to other people — by going out of our way to reject the homosexual, showing our distaste in what we believe to be the strongest form. But here we make the mistake of protesting too much, thereby showing we have something to hide.

In our culture, most of the suffering of homosexuals is quite unnecessary, being due to distaste and contempt for which, by and large, there is no foundation. Not only do these attitudes make for misery, loneliness, difficulty in finding and keeping a job and so on, they also lead to the excesses that in turn provoke public hostility. People who are homosexual are much like anyone else in wanting a circle of friends, young and old, male and female, with whom they associate on a generally nonsexual basis. But they are largely barred from this by social rejection, and are thereby driven to a largely homosexual company of friends. They then seem, and sometimes are, cultish, alien, fundamentally different from other people in ways not having to do with their sexual tastes.

If people who are homosexual could flirt with, woo and win sexual partners in the same unapologetic and public way that heterosexuals do, it is likely that they would be as sexually content as other people are. But being prevented by public prejudice from this matching process, they are sometimes driven to excesses, to displaying their homosexuality conspicuously in the hope of being singled out more readily by others of the same taste, or as an act of defiance against conventional attitudes. They are also driven to hastier and shallower alliances than are possible for people who can pursue their sexual ambitions in a more open and leisurely manner.

Suppose we lived in a rather different world, in which procreation was not only not done in the present way, but not possible in that way, although there were still two sexes, with the present conspicuous biological differences. In this world, we will suppose, pregnancy is effected by taking male semen, refining it chemically in some way, and giving it in pill form to a woman. Suppose further that most people in this world, although they can produce semen if they are male, and become pregnant if they are female, neither experience sexual passion nor derive pleasure from physical contact with other persons; but there are a few exceptions who do have a passionate nature. These people are called "queers." People look on them with distaste and suspicion, and say to one another in shocked tones, "Do you know what they *do* together?" In this world, because things can be very awkward if one makes advances towards someone who is not "queer," and because it is hard to tell who is "queer" and who is not, "queers" develop mannerisms, hairstyles and modes of dress that mark them as such; but this also reveals their proclivities to other people and results in their rejection. So they form little circles of people of their own kind, in which they are thrown together, not because they rejoice in one another as persons—their tastes, talents and interests are as mixed a lot as you would find in any random sample of people — but because of something they would not otherwise have found a significant basis for banding together: their interest in sex. They find their relationships with one another, except in special cases, as unrewarding as one could expect from a very mixed lot of people thrown together by circumstances, and hence find their lives insofar as they depend on enjoying other people, hollow, strained and artificial.

The case is striking because in it we can see how people who would otherwise be regarded as normal, lusty, healthy-minded human beings can, if their eagerness for the opposite sex is treated as queer and distasteful, change and become a breed apart, artificial, dissatisfied with their lives, leary of other people.

It takes a very sober and superior person to keep cool under those pressures, to forgive tormentors, to refrain from excesses, to break down barriers and to carve out a mode of life in which the satisfaction of friendships both of a sexual and a nonsexual kind can be enjoyed. It would help a great deal if even a few people took off the pressure.

We have now discussed many of the questions in the field of sexual morality that are likely to arise for concerned human beings. While answers to most of these questions have been defended, the primary intention has been less to advocate the conclusions than to provide a series of object lessons in the ways in which rational and fruitful deliberations about these matters can be carried on. Although no formula for doing this can be provided, it is still something one can learn; and once learned it can be used, not only to uncover the errors there may be in the reasonings set forth here, but more importantly to cope openly, fairly and at a low emotional temperature with the many moral disagreements we are likely to encounter in the course of an average week.

No small part of the confusion in the position of a moral sceptic can be uncovered by pressing the question: "What are you sceptical of?" It may turn out that the sceptic deplores self-righteousness, thinks reproving and chiding are disagreeable and counter-productive, disagrees with the general run of allegations as to what he should or should not do, or finds most of the arguments he hears about these matters to be a logical morass. Should any or all of these be what he opposes, his scepticism rests on the fundamental mistake of supposing that to be morally concerned is to be self-righteous, to be reproving, to hold such and such views or to conduct one's practical reasoning in certain deplorable ways. It is possible to be morally concerned and to agree with a sceptic in everything he specifically opposes; but if he finds many of the moral arguments he hears laughable, it is no use just saying to him, "I know moral arguments are often of poor quality, and I regret this as much as you do; but they needn't be so poor, and you should take as your target moral argument at its best." One needs also to provide samples of arguments that are not so patently silly. One will then be in a position to say, "There may be defects in these arguments, but they are remediable by the exercise of greater care and discernment, and people who engage in uncovering the defects are not therefore moral sceptics. It is up to you, focussing on moral arguments at their best, to show that even so, criticisms of moral contentions have as little logical traction as arguments intended to support them." Only when we get down to cases in this way is it quite clear what the sceptic's task is; and it is also clear how very difficult it is.

FIVE

How Can We Know the Answers to Moral Questions?

In earlier chapters, especially in chapters 2 and 4, some sustained moral arguments were presented on a number of questions having to do with our sex lives. Someone might read these arguments, and while perhaps finding them faulty in various places, still think that the general manner in which they were conducted was acceptable, and that the errors he found could be corrected by employing the same procedures more thoroughly or more perceptively. He might nevertheless be troubled by some questions that seemed to him more searching. He might for example ask himself: "Although in fact I would deliberate about these matters in largely the same manner, might this be only a cultural accident? Might there not be people who would find this an entirely misguided way of handling these questions, and to whom some quite different way seemed just as right as this way seems to me? For that matter, even if this style of deliberation were everywhere accepted as the sage way to conduct this kind of business, might not our whole concern about these matters be a deplorable obsession that has somehow acquired a hold on the human race? How could one decide about this? We could not say it is a good thing that we should have this concern, because we would then be employing a conception that is part of the concern itself in order to justify it, and that would beg the question."

This is the kind of difficulty with which we will be dealing in this chapter: difficulties having to do, not with the detail of any ground-level moral arguments, but with whether or why we should accept *any* way of deciding these questions.

These are not merely facile if intriguing conundrums, like the question how do we know the world did not come into existence five minutes ago, complete with history books, gravestones, fossils, memories and grandmothers. They are generated quite readily from a little reflection on the moral scene; they are not the inventions of a few ingenious minds, but are widely perceived as problems; and they can be quite debilitating both to individuals and to society's faith in moral reasoning.

There are undoubtedly more difficulties of this bewildering kind than will be taken up here, but if we can allay a few of those that are most natural and most frequently voiced, that may at least provide reason to suppose that other problems of the same sort will likewise prove resolvable.

WHY IS THERE SO MUCH MORAL DISAGREEMENT?

In everyday life the fact that people disagree is tiresome and often saddening, but not in any fundamental way disturbing. If a friend suggests that something I did was unfair, we talk about it, and perhaps I show him that he has misunderstood my action, or he convinces me that I acted hastily and was indeed unfair. Sometimes we will be unable to agree in this way, and that will be disappointing, but we learn to live with such failures, and generally it is more plausible to ascribe them to such causes as not having made our points effectively, than to any fundamental incoherence in the way we deliberate about these matters. Disagreements can be welcomed as helping us to think more honestly about ourselves, or as occasions for upgrading our understanding of one another.

However, when we reflect in a certain way on the panorama of human disagreement, on the fact that conflicting convictions are so widely and persistently held, we may find this not just regrettable, but fundamentally disturbing. We may ask: how are these disagreements to be resolved? If we apply the moral tests used by either of the parties to them, then while that party will come out in the right, the other party will not accept those tests; but if we apply some third set of tests, there will be a problem as to why these should be preferred to the tests accepted by either of the parties. Hence if there is any foundation for anyone's moral convictions, it is at least not now known what it is, and for the time being at least no one can claim any foundation for his beliefs, and they must all be regarded as arbitrary.

Perhaps not many people, in thinking this way, include among the divergences they are contemplating the difference between an average law-abiding citizen and the world's pickpockets, rapists, arsonists and swindlers, but we can make a small start on dismantling the difficulty by noting that there is rarely any disagreement as to what is morally acceptable involved in this difference. The confidence artist's position is not that swindling is not wrongful, but instead either: "I know it is dishonest, but I am going to do it anyway," or if he is exceptionally sophisticated, "I know people call it dishonest, but I don't know what that means." There is also the Robin Hood position that it may be virtuous to steal from the rich and give to the poor, but few of us are certain whether to disagree with that proposition.

We come closer to the root of the problem, however, if we make a distinction between moral convictions and moral reasons. By a moral conviction let us mean a firm view that is adopted and held for a significant length of time as to the general goodness or badness, rightness or wrongness, of a form of behavior, such as gambling, making love with someone else's spouse, helping the needy or keeping a promise. By a moral reason, let us mean anything that might properly be cited in answer to the question why one believes it virtuous to do this, or wrong to do that, such as that it is unfair, dangerous, cruel or deceitful.

It was suggested in the Introduction that some people do not, or do not clearly, have reasons for their convictions. They have been solemnly enjoined not to gamble, and they do not do it, and perhaps disapprove of anyone who does. Having accepted their convictions on someone's authority, they are more likely than others to think it a fair question, "Who is to decide?"; and further, they are more likely to be disquieted by encounters with conflicting convictions, because they have at their disposal nothing more ultimate with which they might deliberate and revise their own. For them, the only question is, "Does this form of behavior diverge from what I believe to be right?"

Clearly if we were all like this it would be difficult to escape the perplexity arising from the contemplation of the panorama of moral disagreement; and it may be suspected that when that perplexity is felt most urgently, the problem is due in large part to having treated diverging convictions as being ultimate, and to meaning by "tests of the convictions" nothing more than whether one of them is in agreement with another.

Most people, however, or most adults, have both convictions and reasons. They find that their moral assessment of some forms of behavior varies so little from case to case that it is unnecessary always to rethink the question whether to act in that way, and a standing moral conviction will serve; but with other recurring questions they may recognize a need to be more flexible, and with highly individual questions they may be entirely inventive.

Now while moral convictions do indeed vary from one person to the next, the theoretical problem to which this gives rise is less acute if the differences are not grossly exaggerated. The problem might be intractable if some people thought it everyone's duty to strangle their second child on its tenth birthday, or thought it profoundly reprehensible to help anyone in distress, and if there were innumerable other differences of conviction just as radical. But in fact, the differences that exist are neither so numerous nor so great as that.

We could make a rough division of moral issues into two kinds: problems to which only one solution seems possible, and problems that need some solution, but might be solved acceptably in quite a variety of different ways. The problem of personal security seems to require prohibitions against killing, assault and theft, and while we know of societies in which the newborn are sometimes killed, or the very aged, we can scarcely imagine a society in which all killings, assaults and thefts were a matter of indifference. On the other hand, in the fields of business ethics or sexual morality, while it is desirable to have some understandings that enable us to carry on our affairs in a livable way, there can be a variety of different arrangements that are more or less equally workable. Hence in these areas, while it may not be at all morally necessary that we should have a certain practice rather than some alternative to it, it may yet be of considerable importance whether, having that practice, we act as it requires.

Regardless of where one looks, there are not in fact wide divergences in people's convictions concerning questions basic to personal security; and while in such areas as business ethics and sexual morality the differences can be quite striking, we can now see that it is not a problem that there should be such differences, since there is no reason to expect that everyone should have devised the same ways of handling questions of this kind.

If we confine our attention to the differences that exist within one culture, it may be suggested that they are normally very much smaller than may appear from the fact that some people will say yes to a question like, "Was that an irresponsible thing to do?" while others will say no. What greater difference could there be? Yet if we take a typical actual case, we will find that the disputants are not far apart. Is it irresponsible to put up a large satellite, pieces of which might conceivably do grave damage when its orbit finally disintegrates if (a) no mechanism is built into it by which the location of its return to earth can be controlled, (b) it is anticipated that before it is ready to crash, a means will have been developed of sending it into outer space, and (c) even if this does not happen, the chance of its causing serious damage is extremely small? People disagree vehemently on such questions, but each recognizes the force of the other's argument, and the vehemence is due mostly to the fact that the disputants are so close together. They wish to emphasize a fine, but as it seems to them, important difference. They agree in their fundamental way of thinking about such questions, and disagree on the fine points of its application to particular cases.

If we turn from the varying convictions we may find, to the ways of thinking underlying the convictions, we do not find striking divergences. No one thinks that such questions as "What harm would it do?", "Whose rights would it violate?", "To whom would it be unfair?" or "Is it likely to misinform?" are morally irrelevant. As was suggested earlier, there are people who do not learn to ask these questions, but they do not disagree as to their relevance. For them the question has not yet arisen, and they hold no view about it.

When we bring these questions to bear on a particular case, difficulties can arise, and it is rarely possible to claim that only one decision is justifiable, but that would tend to show that our moral thinking is a morass only if it frequently happened that one person concluded that a course of action was altogether excellent, while another decided that it was utterly abominable. Such wide divergences do not in fact occur, and when one person recommends for and another against a proposed action, they may be close together, in the sense that the person opposed recognizes what counts in favor of the action, but thinks it insufficient, and the person advocating the action recognizes what counts against it, but thinks it is outweighed by the favorable considerations.

Since moral decisions can be complicated matters, it is to be expected that this much variation in them should be common, and hence the fact that we disagree in this way is no cause for alarm or scepticism.

The argument here has relied heavily on a distinction between convictions and reasons. The validity of this distinction might be questioned, but its defence is a somewhat abstruse matter, and will be left to an appendix.

WHY IS MORAL REASONING SO OFTEN INCONCLUSIVE?

A different, if related, source of overriding perplexity arises from the fact that, even within one way of thinking about moral problems, there are many cases in which no one conclusion as to what to do seems very clearly to be preferred to various alternatives. Here the problem is not so much that people disagree as that, if I have done A in a case of this kind and someone else says he would have done B, we may both quite soon see that neither of us has anything decisive to say in support of his view.

Reflecting on this we may despairingly come to fear that the known forms of moral reasoning, however convincing they may seem to us at times, are a fundamentally ineffective instrument, and that the real determinants of our decisions are not the deliberations we go through, but something else, not commanding the same respect — conditioning, perhaps, or personal preference.

The kind of case in which this inconclusiveness most often appears occurs when there are some considerations counting for and others counting against a proposed line of action, and when the same is true of every other course of action we consider. If some action is quite likely to be beneficial to some people, but entails a certain risk to others, and if I also could not perform it without failing to keep a promise I have made, but on the other hand it may not be very important to the person to whom I so promised whether I keep the promise or not, there will be much room for disagreement as to what to do. At such times we would dearly like to have at our disposal ways of balancing one consideration against another: of deciding how much likely benefit rightly outweighs how much risk of harm, how much difference it makes whether the people likely to suffer are different from those likely to gain, just when an opportunity to confer a benefit entitles us to break a promise, or when it matters whether the person to whom a promise was made would not be seriously disadvantaged if the promise were not kept. Yet while some people may adopt guidelines for such cases which they feel to be fair, there are no well-recognized rules for deciding these questions, and there seems no way of showing that one rule is preferable to another.

One might plausibly conclude from this that moral reasoning is a morass, because it lacks mechanisms for answering the many questions it raises of how to balance one thing against another. One way of solving this problem might be to contrive a new way of deciding these questions, so designed as to yield a clear conclusion in every kind of case. That, however, seems foredoomed to failure, for the following reason: if a mechanism is produced that makes every moral question decidable, there will still be a question whether the decisions it generates are morally sound. This question cannot be answered by checking over the working of the mechanism in particular cases to see if mistakes have been made, because it is a question whether, when functioning correctly, the mechanism generates sound decisions. It can therefore be answered only by seeing whether what the mechanism yields agrees with what we get when thinking as carefully as possible in the ordinary way; but if ordinary moral thinking yields no decision in cases where the mechanism does, there will be that much divergence between ordinary thinking and thinking under the new system, and the latter will to that extent be shown to be defective. In short, to whatever extent the invented mechanism achieves its end of making otherwise undecidable questions decidable, it shows itself to be ethically defective.

Hence instead of trying to solve the problem, we might better see if it can be *dissolved*. The following points may at least contribute to its dissolution:

1. While there are some cases in which undecidability seems to loom large, and we tend to fasten on them, they are not after all so very typical. In the course of an average month most of the decisions we take are not infected with this difficulty.

2. When the problem does arise, it is fair to suggest that the morally sound attitude, whichever decision is taken, is one of

diffidence or of mixed feelings. We are not bound in every case to judge an action unqualifiedly good or bad, right or wrong; and the judgment that it has this to be said for it, but that to be said against it may be fully warranted.

3. It is not clear, given the previous point, that we need the suggested rules for mediating between conflicting considerations, which we seemed bound to regard as matters of personal preference, but if we do sometimes need them, or if some people anyway use them, they could not fundamentally alter the moral complexion of the problem. If they resulted in our choosing one of a set of contemplated alternatives where otherwise we might have chosen differently, still they will hardly show that the course chosen is excellent and without fault, if otherwise it would not have appeared so.

4. Very often in this kind of case, greater moral seriousness may lead to devising a solution which *is* clearly warranted. In describing the example on pages 149-50, the solutions contemplated were limited and uninventive, and it was by restricting ourselves to these dullard's solutions that the appearance of fundamental undecidability was generated. Faced with that problem, a more comprehensive solution might have been devised. For example, the decision might be (a) to do the thing likely to be beneficial, (b) to take steps to avoid the risk of harm, (c) if harm did anyway result, to provide adequate compensation to those who had suffered it, (d) to seek the consent of the person to whom a promise had been made, to break it, and (e) to compensate that person for any loss thereby suffered.

The sceptical argument here is plausible only if we greatly overstate the inconclusiveness of our ways of thinking about moral questions. The extent and degree of inconclusiveness that we actually find is quite to be expected, and is no cause for alarm. The means we have for deciding, while they will leave us uncertain in some cases, are not therefore useless, especially if we employ them with some vigor and care.

HOW CAN MORAL REASONS BE JUSTIFIED?

A somewhat different sceptical argument might be stated as follows: we can justify our moral convictions with arguments relating to moral reasons, but either the moral reasons we give are not themselves justifiable, or if they are, that is done by reference to further considerations which again are either not themselves justifiable or . . . and so on. Although there is conceivably a hierarchy of reasons, we are not in fact able to carry it to more than perhaps three or four levels; and whatever level we may reach, the considerations cited at that level still stand in need of a justification. Moreover, there appears to be an inherent impossibility of giving a moral justification of any moral reasons that are at all basic: it is question-begging to argue that it is good or fair or honest to count such-and-such as reasons, yet any other considerations on which we might rely, whatever they show, will not show that we are right in what we count as moral reasons. Such other considerations could not show this, because, being other, they are not moral considerations. Hence it appears that our moral reasons are incapable of being given a justification, and must be regarded as arbitrary or as matters of personal choice.

The objector here sees a model of moral justification in the way we argue that actions are acceptable since they are neither cruel, dangerous, selfish, unfair or dishonest, and requires that there should be a similar justification for such ways of deciding these questions. At the same time he rightly points out the impossibility of such a justification, since if it employed moral conceptions it would be question-begging, while if it did not, it would not be a moral justification.

It is not very clear, however, that there is a need for what he is demanding. Generally, if it can be shown that it would be logically impossible to satisfy a requirement, that is a very good reason for not requiring it; but this demand might still be reasonable if there were striking differences in what people counted as moral reasons, and there was therefore a need for some way of deciding between them. We do not, however, find, for example, that while many people count the fact that an action is cruel or dangerous as a reason for thinking it immoral, others treat these questions as quite irrelevant to that issue.

There are, however, various features of the moral scene that might at least generate the illusion that this kind of disagreement was common:

1. There are people who have no concern about moral issues and, except from the point of view of prudence, do not care whether an action is cruel, harmful, unfair, deceitful and so on. As noted earlier, however, they do not hold that cruelty is morally acceptable. The question what is morally acceptable plays no part in their practical thinking, and they have no opinions about it.

2. Many people are prepared to say in special cases that actions are morally recommendable in spite of being deceitful, unfair, dangerous and so on. It may appear that they are treating these considerations as irrelevant, at least in certain cases, but they are not: they recognize the danger or the deception as counting against the action, but think it outweighed by other considerations.

3. Some of the conceptions we use in moral reasoning are themselves unclear. What one counts as unfair, for example, may depend on when or where one was brought up; and although there might be agreement that if anything is unfair, that counts against it, there might be little agreement from case to case as to what in particular is to be called unfair. For example, it used to be said that it is fair that a person doing a job requiring unusual intelligence and extensive training should be more highly paid than one doing a job requiring only average intelligence and relatively little training; however, that conviction is not so widely held now.

It is perhaps by dwelling on such examples, that doubts may be engendered as to whether our views on what is fair are altogether subjective; but these examples may be misleading in at least the following ways:

1. Many cases are not so arguably matters of opinion. For

example, if two people are equally capable and diligent, and have been employed by a company for the same length of time, there is not much room for argument as to whether it is fair to pay one of them more money because he presses more strenuously for raises in pay.

2. It was not decided on as a fair policy that doctors, for example, should be more highly paid than electricians. The argument that doctors deserve higher pay because their work requires greater intelligence and training may be regarded as an after-the-event rationalization of a state of affairs that happens to prevail. There are clear questions of fairness concerning the monetary rewards given two electricians by one employer, or two doctors, but it is not clear that we know how to decide whether it is fair that doctors should be more generously rewarded than electricians.

3. The question whether something is fair tends, more than the questions whether something is deceitful or cruel, to fall into the category of cases where it is desirable to have some solution to a social problem, but various solutions may be equally workable. It is desirable, for example, that people should know what they have to do if they want salary increases, and fair that people complying with the understood conditions should be rewarded accordingly; but we can imagine quite different sets of such conditions prevailing at different times or places, between which, if there is anything to choose morally, it is not on the grounds of fairness. The fairness comes in, not in the choice of conditions, but in the administration of the conditions currently applying. It may be very clear whether the existing understandings about how employees are to be rewarded have been fairly administered. If some companies pay their staff on a piece-work basis, and others by the hour, it is not at all clear whether the question even arises whether one policy is fairer than another, but still both companies may be fair or unfair in the way they administer their respective policies.

So far, the reply to the sceptical argument in this section has consisted, not in satisfying the demand it makes for a justification of moral reasons, but in suggesting that there would be a need for such a justification only if there were fundamental disagreements between people in what they counted as moral reasons, and that in fact there are not such disagreements. The semblance of disagreement that there may be in certain kinds of cases arises from misunderstandings of what is going on in those cases.

In earlier chapters, we had occasion to consider two other kinds of cases which might also be relevant in this context: cases in which someone wants to add to the list of considerations properly affecting a moral decision, and possible disagreements as to whether something which was agreed to be regrettable or defective was *morally* regrettable or defective. The argument that the practice of birth control is immoral because unnatural was treated as attempting to add being unnatural to the stock of considerations properly affecting a moral decision; and the question was discussed whether relating to people on an impersonal basis, if it is sometimes regrettable, counts as a moral fault. The way of handling these questions that was proposed need not be repeated here.

An objector might see his difficulty as having been relieved but not removed by the argument so far on this topic. He might persist: "But after all, how do we *know* that the fact that something is cruel, dangerous or unfair is a reason for thinking it immoral? Even if everyone who is not a moral sceptic agrees about this, or if any disagreements that exist can be shown to arise from confusions, might we not all still be making a fundamental mistake?"

It would be clearer that the difficulty expressed here was coherent if, quite independently of such concepts as cruelty, harm, unfairness, deception and so on (or their opposites), we knew what the word "moral" meant, and if we had devised the questions "Is it unfair?", "Is it cruel?" and so on, as ways of deciding in particular cases whether actions were morally acceptable. Then raising this difficulty would be like asking how we know that our ways of deciding whether distant stars are receding are reliable. In the latter case we know, independently of these methods, what it means to say that a star is receding at such and such a rate, and it is a fair question whether we might have made a mistake in settling on the methods we use for deciding this.

In the moral case it is different, however. "Immoral" does not have a meaning quite independent of our methods of establishing it, and therefore there is no possibility of showing that we have made a mistake in our choice of methods.

It might be different if "immoral"'certainly meant "displeasing to God" but, having no direct information as to God's pleasure, we had committed ourselves to the hunch that among the things that displease Him are the cruel, the dishonest, the unfair, and so on. Certainly someone might then ask how we know this is how God's preferences run; and we might have to answer that so far it is only a guess and a gamble.

As things stand, however, we do not attach that sense to the word "immoral." We may believe that God is displeased by what is immoral, but in so thinking we would be defining the immoral in some other way, otherwise we would only be saying that God is displeased by what displeases Him.

If, neither in the way just considered nor in any other, does the word "immoral" have sense independently of the ways we have of deciding what is immoral, the question cannot arise whether we might have adopted the wrong ways of deciding; and we can say, "I don't know what 'immoral' would mean, if the fact that an action was cruel, dangerous, unfair or deceitful did not count as reasons for saying it was immoral."

A difficulty still remains, however. It was argued that "immoral" has to be defined in terms of the ways we have of deciding what is immoral; but are there not different ways of deciding, and hence, according to this argument, different meanings for this word? Can we not therefore simply rephrase the question to read, What reason can we have for adopting this meaning, rather than that, for this word?

As now worded, the question is somewhat strange, but the blame for that lies rather in the course of our argument than in anyone's natural inclination to express a difficulty in these terms, so we can only make do with what we ourselves have created. Two main points may be offered:

1. There are indeed various ways of deciding these questions, and much of our discussion, especially in chapters 1 to 4, has been an evaluation of conflicting ways. One way of deciding is by whether something is at variance with one's convictions, and a person who thought that way might say, "Such and such is wrong because it is gambling"; but it was argued that no reason, or no sufficient reason, is given here, because there is a meaningful question whether gambling is wrong.

In a different kind of case it was argued that to say, "Birth control is wrong because it is unnatural" is unsatisfactory, both because whether something is unnatural is not one of the recognized questions to ask, and because the proponents of the argument take no exception to other practices that are unnatural in just as good a sense. In short, it is not after all, as the objection took it to be, a rhetorical question what reason there can be for choosing between ways of deciding. Numerous examples of such reasons have been provided here.

2. Only in a few cases is it possible to say that we would be at a loss, and would lose our grip on the concept of morality, if a specific consideration were not a reason for thinking something right or wrong, good or bad. There are points at which we thus reach rock bottom, and others at which, although we may try saying we would be at a loss, it can soon be shown that there are in fact ways in which further reflection may be carried on. We can ask and answer the question what is wrong with wanting to flourish without working, but if we ask what is wrong with cruelty, then while a multitude of reasons may flood to mind, they turn out either to be covert elucidations of what cruelty is (for example, "It results in suffering"), or at any rate to be attempts to base what is more certain on what is less so. What happens here is that, having so little doubt that cruelty is wrong, we think there must be very strong reasons for so believing; but this proposition is one of the

foundations of our moral thinking, and there can hardly be foundations for the foundations. That is not to say that they are unfounded — that is, that they lack something proper to a moral assertion — but rather the requirement that they be founded does not apply to foundations, but only to what is built on them.

The practical importance of this is that if anyone were seriously to ask what is wrong with cruelty, we make a fundamental mistake if we goodheartedly try to give him his reasons, in the way we might if he had asked, for example, what is wrong with paying an ignorant person much less than the market value for his goods, if he is willing to sell them at that price. Rather, we should tell him that he does not understand moral thinking, and needs lessons in it, if he is in doubt about whether an action's being cruel makes it wrong.

In the lessons he might be shown how we deliberate about various kinds of questions, but we would not be *arguing* that this is the way to go about it, but rather informing him of it, and training him in it. If he proved an able student, he might soon reach a level of competence where he could successfully challenge some of the fine points in the teaching, but on such questions as whether cruelty or dishonesty is a moral defect, our position would have to be that if he contemplates negative answers, he thereby shows that he has not yet learned how this thinking is done, and needs more training. The propositions that cruelty and dishonesty are moral faults are part of the equipment for deciding, and are not among the questions that are up for decision.

IS RATIONAL PERSUASION POSSIBLE?

Some of the points just made may provide a way of resolving another difficulty that has perplexed some people, and led them to despair of the possibility of usefully discussing moral disagreements. The problem is that, while people's attitudes may be changed by threats and ridicule and psychological conditioning, to persuade anyone of anything by an argument, it will be necessary to appeal to premises already accepted. It will be no use, for example, to argue against a course of action by detailing the harm that is likely to result, unless the other person is already satisfied that the fact that an action will be harmful is a reason against doing it. It follows from this that while we can rationally persuade people of minor points here and there, perhaps by pointing out kinds of harm they might not have expected, no fundamental changes could be brought about by rational means, since if the fundamental things were not already accepted, there would be no accepted premises on which they could be based.

Anyone who accepted this extremely plausible line of reasoning would of course despair of any rational approach to serious differences of moral opinion, and would perhaps resort to oratory, threats, insinuations, ridicule or conditioning. Yet if we are rational enough to find these tactics offensive, and many people are, they will not work either, but will instead contribute to social estrangement and hostility.

It is possible simply to ignore these theoretical difficulties and proceed to discuss moral issues that arise as best one can, letting the persuasiveness of the activity be as it may. If, in spite of the above considerations, anyone is ever persuaded of a fundamental point, that may suggest that there must be something wrong with the reasoning that shows this to be impossible; but *what* is wrong could be treated as an academic question to be considered some time at one's leisure. However, we do not need to let the matter rest there, because the difficulty can in fact quite readily be resolved.

When we propound an argument to show that this would be unfair or that would be harmful, we are relying on the assumption that what is unfair or harmful is (at least in the absence of countervailing considerations) wrong; but we are not assuming that the other person believes this, but rather that, whether or not he believes it, it cannot reasonably be denied. What we are doing is not like saying, "You Christians believe in forgiveness, so how can you favor capital punishment?" where whether or not we ourselves believe in forgiveness, we are using others' belief in it to persuade them of something we may believe in for other reasons. Instead we are saying, "I don't know whether you believe that the fact that an action would be harmful is a reason against doing it, but it is, and therefore (unless there are countervailing considerations) this action would be wrong."

Contrary to what is often assumed, an argument under these terms could succeed in being persuasive. In this kind of case we instruct another person about a feature of moral thinking, and show that when applied to the question at hand, the result is such and such. Some people will resist such instruction, but there is no reason to suppose that everyone will. In practice, to be sure, it will be a very rare person who is not already acquainted with the point on which we are supposing instruction to be offered. Other people, we could say, may sometimes need to be reminded of a point of morals which they might not, of their own accord, have brought into play; but the people, if such there be, to whom the instruction is new need not accept it on the personal authority of whoever acts as their teacher. They may ask around, and find that no one dissents; or they may, by reflecting on various moral deliberations they have overheard, realize that what they were told is indeed a fair statement of part of the way these questions are decided.

So far we have been supposing that the question about which two people are arguing is just as to whether some action is morally recommendable. In practice, when someone asks, "Should I do this?", it may not be very clear to him what his problem is. He may be in part asking such questions as, "If this is wrong, is that a reason for me not to do it?", or "Are there any advantages in my doing (or not doing) this that might reconcile me to doing (or not doing) it?" When those questions hover in the wings, the issue will be fundamentally confused, and a point that makes a genuine contribution to one of the questions may nevertheless seem wide of the mark, because the person who asked what he should do is not clear what his problem is, and the point fails to cope with other aspects of his difficulty.

This kind of crux is by no means unmanageable, however. One may begin by sorting out the questions, suggesting, for example, that the questioner may want to know either (a) whether the suggested action would be wrong, (b) whether, if it was wrong, that is a reason for not doing it, or (c) whether his doing it would have advantages for him that might reconcile him to it.

The second step would be to find out which of these questions stated the problem. The answer might be only (a) or only (c), or some pair of them, or all of them. Of these, the alternative we can most usefully consider is all three. Given that answer, one could proceed in this way:

1. One could show, in the ways already sufficiently canvassed, whether or how far the suggested action was morally recommendable. For simplicity's sake, let us suppose that the indications here are quite clearly negative.

2. Turning then to the question whether the fact that the action was wrong is a reason not to do it, one could make the point that to show that an action is wrong *is* to show that it should not be done. When we have reached the conclusion that an action would be wrong, there is no question, about which further moral deliberation is possible, whether to do it. We have already answered the moral questions, "What harm would it do?", "Whose rights would be violated?", "To whom would it be unfair?" and further deliberations clearly could not take us beyond the moral conclusion and bridge the supposed gap between the question whether something is wrong and the question whether to do it.

In arguing in this way that there is no moral question here, one would not be saying that it makes no sense to ask, "But shall I do it?", but only that it makes no *moral* sense. The only moral reasons for doing the right thing are the reasons that show it to be right.

Perhaps someone might not accept the point that has been elaborated here, and require to be persuaded of it. Quite clearly we could not provide him with the reasons he demands. It is among the rock-bottom points of morals, and would have to be presented as such. We would have to put it that a person cannot think about moral questions if he does not accept this.

3. Since it is often supposed that no one will ever do anything unless he believes it to be in his interest, the question, "What are the advantages?" may seem the hardest of all, and may seem always to need a convincing answer. It is not clear, however, whether this supposition is true, and it may be a mistake to raise the question as to the advantages, except with such persons as fairly clearly treat it as decisive.

When the question does need to be dealt with, there is a danger of handling it in such a way as to allow the issue to hinge on whether the advantages are sufficient, and one must begin by saying that, from a moral point of view, whether to do something does not depend on its advantages. There may very often be advantages, many of which, in the heat of a moment, are easily overlooked, but many virtuous acts or abstentions are either altogether to the disadvantage of the person performing them, or promise losses out of all proportion to any likely gains; and the question whether an act is wrong or right is quite unaffected by advantages or disadvantages attending its performance.

In a few special cases, for example, where the person acting is one of the parties to whom the action may be fair or unfair, the question of the advantage to oneself may be relevant to a decision as to what it is right or best to do, but only indirectly: by being fair to oneself, an advantage may accrue. Even so, it is not because it is advantageous, but because it is fair, that the action is morally recommendable. This comes out clearly in the case in which fairness to oneself is disadvantageous.

Having made the point that the decision cannot properly hinge on the advantages, one may sometimes usefully enlarge on the advantages, or suggest ways in which the disadvantages may be minimized. Once the prudential questions have been isolated in the way outlined, the discussion of them is unlikely to generate philosophical perplexity, but difficulties might arise over the way of isolating them. Someone might demand a reason why prudential considerations are, with some minor exceptions, irrelevant to moral decisions.

There is perhaps this reason: the questions, "What is virtuous?" and "What is prudent?" are distinct. Each is to be decided in its own way. It may be, as some moralists have plausibly maintained, that the decisions made in these different ways coincide in a surprisingly large number of cases, but only by divine intervention could they conceivably coincide in every case. In fact they do diverge; but if a moral question could be decided by prudential considerations, in any case in which there was an apparent divergence, we would have to conclude that we had made some mistake in our moral reasoning; and if we were entitled to that conclusion in every case, we could dispense with moral thinking, and prudential thinking would suffice. Since, however, our prudential reasoning so frequently yields conclusions apparently at variance with our moral reasoning, we would still need, as a check on the thoroughness of the former, a way of reaching moral conclusions. Then if our prudential thinking did not lead us to the same conclusion, we would know we had made some mistake in it, and could rethink it until it came out right. It turns out now, however, that we only need moral reasoning. If we know by the conclusion it yields whether we have made a mistake in our prudential thinking, it will be only out of curiosity that we rethink it until we get the required conclusion. Thus we are landed in an impossible muddle by the supposition that moral questions can be decided by prudential means.

Rational persuasion is undoubtedly a difficult business, and is not often successful, but we have now argued that it is not owing to any theoretical impossibility that it is so often disappointing. It seems more likely on the whole that its tendency to fail is due to the conditions in which it is carried on. Few of us are very skilled at it. There is frequently not enough time to canvass the issues thoroughly. We are often too emotionally involved to attend carefully to the argument. The participants are usually an aggrieved party and someone against whom he has made a complaint, and so on. If we curbed our despairing thoughts about it and tried it more often, we might all improve our capacity to persuade and to be persuaded.

A TACTICAL SHORTCUT

So far in this chapter, ways have been suggested in which, if there were all the time in the world, various kinds of overriding objection to a ground-level moral contention could be argued out. It should be pointed out that it need not always be necessary in this way to stop in our tracks while we settle, or perhaps more likely fail to settle, this kind of difficulty. Consider the following exchange:

"I don't think homosexuality is immoral. Homosexuals, like anyone else, may be unkind to one another, or unfair or deceitful, but it is not by being homosexual that they are so, and their lovemaking can be, and normally is, free of these and any other moral defects you care to mention."

"That is just your opinion."

"Of course it is my opinion. If it were not, I would not have defended it; and if I did not know that other people disagreed, I would not bother arguing for it. The question is, am I right?"

"But what I am saying is that one can't argue about these things."

"Can't one? I just have. If there is something wrong with my argument, it is up to you to show that there is; but if you do, you will at the same time be showing that we can argue about these things. So come now, consider my argument, and stop talking about whether to do so."

Not every sceptic would be quieted in this way, but some might; and it is not clear that anyone who was thereby induced to participate in some moral deliberation would be a victim of sophistry.

A CONTRAST WITH SOME
PHILOSOPHICAL APPROACHES

The procedure followed in the practical deliberations in earlier chapters was that of giving miscellaneous everyday reasons for the moral evaluations of forms of behavior that were defended. It is an amorphous and somewhat inconclusive procedure, but if used with some vigor, skill and care, it is by no means useless. We list a number of rather different features, the possession of any one of which will be a reason for thinking an action morally recommendable or otherwise. Perplexities can arise when some of the features of an action are morally favorable, and others morally adverse, but difficulties of this kind do not beset every moral question we face, and they are not unresolvable. Very often when there is this kind of conflict, the indicated conclusion is not a flat recommendation for or against a proposed course of action, but in effect a summary of the favorable and adverse considerations: the action would be good in these ways, but not in those. Given such a summary, some people will decide to do the proposed action, while others will incline against doing it; but they need not be far apart in their evaluations, and the distance can be reduced in practice by such means as taking steps to minimize the disadvantages, or to compensate the persons to whom they accrue.

By proceeding on this basis, we can manage without taking a stand on the questions that have always interested philosophers as to the ultimate basis of morality. Theorists interested in ultimate questions try to find some one reason why all the various considerations we employ in making moral decisions are treated as moral reasons. Utilitarians, for example, try to show that honesty, courage, fairness and generosity are all good for the one reason that they are conducive to happiness.

It will make no difference to us whether they are right about this, because it will still be true that honesty, courage, fairness and generosity are good things, and there need be no divergence between us and utilitarians in our attitudes towards gambling, boozing, drug use or promiscuity. Perhaps if we think honesty is good both in itself and for its happiness-producing or misery-lessening tendencies, while utilitarians think it good only for these tendencies, there will be some minor differences in the pattern of our decisions in cases where these values come into conflict; but these differences will probably be smaller than the differences between one utilitarian and another over the same range of questions. Neither utilitarianism nor any other moral theory that has ever been devised is conspicuous for the conclusiveness of the practical decisions it yields.

Now let us make a different supposition: that it turns out that utilitarians cannot show that the happiness-producing tendencies of fairness are at all sufficient to account for the importance we attach to it. The questions would then arise, is fairness overrated, or is utilitarianism an inadequate theory? The question is difficult, but one thing that seems clear is that if the project is to construct a theory accounting for the importance attached to all the various things to which it *is* attached, then any theory that fails in that endeavor is inadequate. Of course, it is not certain that that *is* the project, but on the one hand it is certainly very often so treated, and on the other it is very difficult to suggest in what other way a theory of that kind could be justified.

Utilitarianism has been used as an example here, but Kantianism or anything else that addressed itself to the same task would do just as well. The important thing is that if the argument of the preceding paragraph is sound, then it cannot possibly make any difference to us *how* inquiries into the ultimate basis of morality turn out, since they will always be accounting for just the things we are treating as the determinants of moral questions. In addition, ours will generally be the more comprehensive approach, since those who seek ultimate reasons will be under a perennial temptation to discount anything that cannot readily be fitted into their theories, and any yielding to that temptation will distort moral thinking and restrict its variety.

Perhaps the main motivation for these ultimate inquiries is a question like this: we think that an action is wrong insofar as it is dangerous, and given that way of thinking we have a reason for saying that such and such actions are wrong, but do we not in turn need a reason for adopting this way of deciding these questions, rather than some other way? It is not difficult to see, however, that if the need that is expressed here for a prior justification is genuine, there will be the same need for a justification of any justification that may be suggested, and so on indefinitely. It would be a very interesting fact, certainly, if all the different reasons we give in different cases for our moral evaluations could be reduced to one reason, but without a theory that a successful generalization is itself a justification, the reduction of various reasons to one has no tendency to provide a foundation for those reasons. If we were in serious doubt as to whether the fact that a proposed action would be dishonest is a reason for thinking it would be wrong, we could equally doubt whether the fact that it was conducive to unhappiness, or the fact that it would be unacceptable to have everyone act that way, is a reason for thinking it would be wrong. Many of us do in fact readily enough accept the utilitarian or the Kantian principles, at least to the extent of not finding them patently misguided, whatever reservations we may have regarding the fine points. But we do not accept these theories more fully than we accept the propositions that insofar as an action would be unfair, or insofar as it would be selfish, it would be wrong.

CONCLUSION

Attempts by philosophers to come to grips directly with human problems have traditionally been regarded as makeshift efforts, which may be excusable as interim measures until the fundamental problems of ethical theory are solved, but which, lacking the grounding ultimately to be provided by ethical theory, cannot be much better than the "disgusting medley of compiled observations and half-reasoned principles" which Kant derided, and from which, he said, "[m]en of insight . . . avert their eyes."*

Against this it may be suggested that however contemptible popular moral philosophy may sometimes be, it is neither inevitably so, nor is its salvation to be found only in some theoretical grounding, whether of the kind Kant proposed, or as provided by some theory that would compete with his.

If in this chapter we have dissolved some theoretical perplexities about the grounds of moral convictions, we have satisfied the demand Kant made upon popular philosophy; not, however, by providing a theory that might succeed where Kant's theory failed, but by showing his demand to be unwarranted.

A new conception of moral philosophy has been elaborated here, one in which concrete moral issues are discussed unapologetically, and in which what is distinctively philosophical about those deliberations is their presentation in such a way as to accentuate the modes of thinking that are being deployed. The need for this lies, not in the fact that these modes of thinking are a philosophical discovery that, being new, has to be taught, but in the fact that what we learn about moral thinking as we grow up can be extremely confusing when applied to complicated or unfamiliar cases. We lose our way, and attribute the problems we have, not to our own want of skill in handling these matters, but to imperfections in the method itself. One of the main practical benefits philosophy can confer is that of restoring confidence in the method by providing illustrations of how, with a little skill in its use, it can be made to cope with the hard questions too.

Fundamental Principles of the Metaphysic of Morals, translated by T. K. Abbott, Longmans Green and Co., London, 1889, p. 26.

APPENDIX

The Distinction between Moral Reasons and Moral Convictions

A distinction on which many of the arguments of this book have relied is that between moral convictions and moral reasons. Nothing need hinge on the choice of terminology here. Instead of convictions we could just as well speak of beliefs, opinions, conclusions or perhaps stances, and instead of reasons we might equally speak of principles or criteria. By a moral conviction is meant here any settled view as to what sorts of actions are permissible, commendable, deplorable, unacceptable or a duty, or settled views as to the circumstances in which an action is commendable, deplorable, and so on. By a moral reason is meant anything to which we appeal in defending a moral conviction; for example when we show that an action was fair or beneficial, or harmful, cruel or deceitful.

While the distinction has many uses in moral deliberations, doubts may arise as to its defensibility. Some people treat what we might otherwise call a conviction as a reason; for example, if they argue that buying lottery tickets is wrong because it is gambling, or that "free love" is wrong because it is sexual activity outside of marriage. Here the distinction we want to draw seems to collapse. Again, if there are hierarchies of moral reasons, as in the argument that gambling is wrong because it fosters the hope of prospering without working, and prospering without working is wrong because our survival requires work, and it is unfair that work should be unequally distributed, any intermediate thesis in the hierarchy will appear as a reason when it is used in defending a lower thesis, but as a conviction when it is itself being defended. Here again the distinction seems to collapse.

These difficulties are quite easily set aside, however, by the following arguments:

1. Whether something is a reason is not a question of whether someone, or everyone, so treats it, but of whether it serves the purpose of justifying. For example, it does not serve that purpose to argue that buying lottery tickets is wrong because it is gambling. If we are seriously raising the question whether the former is wrong, we are at the same time raising that question about the latter. To be told that it is gambling conveys no new information about buying lottery tickets, and therefore the moral question is not affected by that point.

2. It is different in the case of hierarchies. It does shed new light on gambling to be told that it fosters the hope of prospering without working, and so does contribute to a justification of the view that it is wrong. Still, the new light contributed is of a factual, not an evaluative, nature, and the moral point does not emerge until we get to the claim that it is unfair that some people should prosper without working. (The argument here, incidentally, is used strictly as an illustration, and there is no intention to endorse it.) Even if an intermediate thesis in a hierarchy of reasons sometimes includes a distinctively moral point, it will not be objectionable to call the thesis a conviction insofar as it is further justifiable, but a reason insofar as it justifies a lower thesis.

We argue that a proposed action would be wrong because it would be cruel: why would we not call it a *conviction* one may have that the fact that an action would be cruel is a reason for thinking it would be wrong?

We do not exactly *believe* that cruelty or deception is wrong. Not that we disbelieve it, or are in doubt about it, or know it either; but to say, "I believe that so-and-so" is to take a stand, while at the same time expressly recognizing that one might be wrong. We cannot treat the wrongness of cruelty in that way as a matter of opinion. As suggested earlier, only if we had a clear concept of the immoral, which was quite distinct from the cruel, the unfair, the deceptive, and so on, would it make sense to treat as debatable and needing to be shown that cruelty is wrong. If someone is cruel without a qualm, he is not of a different opinion from most of us about whether cruelty is morally permissible, he just takes no interest in that question.

We have moral convictions about actions or types of action which, being described in morally neutral terms, can therefore, as far as their description goes, meaningfully be adjudged virtuous or otherwise. If murder is the wrongful killing of a human being, we cannot ask whether murder is wrong; but we can ask whether killing a human being is wrong, because the latter description is morally neutral.

Someone who altogether disapproves of gambling or wife-swapping may use those expressions as if they were evaluative terms, that is, charge them with his disapprobation, and see no need to say that they are wrong; but still they are not evaluative expressions. It is not redundant to say that wife-swapping is wrong, or contradictory to say that it is morally acceptable.

Whereas it would merely be repeating oneself to say that when Paul started living with Peter's wife and Peter with Paul's, they swapped wives, and would not tell us anything about the moral character of the arrangement, it would be morally informative to say that it was unfair to Peter to pay him less than Paul. That an action was unfair, cruel or dishonest does not itself decide whether it is wrong. Actions may be morally recommendable although unfair, and morally regrettable although beneficial, if there are considerations both for and against and one seems to outweigh the other. What we are calling moral reasons will not always decide a question, but they do make a contribution to deciding, and one that needs no further justification.

We can justify the claim that something was unfair — for

example, by saying that Paul had worked just as hard as Peter —
but we cannot justify the claim that if or insofar as it was unfair, it
was wrong; that is, that its unfairness counts against its being
morally recommendable. Not that this claim is *unjustifiable*; that
is, in need of but lacking a justification. In deciding that anything is
unfair, we have decided that there is something against it morally.
It makes no sense to say, "I agree it was unfair, but I wonder if
there was anything wrong with it." One can, however, say of some
actions that they ought to be done in spite of their unfairness. In
such a case their unfairness is still a moral fault, but not one grave
enough to decide against the performance of the action.

A test of whether a word expresses a moral reason is whether it
will fit in the sentence, "It was ————, but I wonder whether
there was anything wrong with it (or good about it)." If it does *not*
fit, it expresses a reason. What it is a reason *for* is believing an
action to be immoral, right, wrong, a duty, and so on. These latter
words do not of course express moral reasons, that is to say reasons
for thinking actions immoral, right, wrong, a duty and so on; but
they may still be used in giving reasons of another kind, namely
reasons for doing or refraining from an action. "I thought it was
immoral because it was wrong" is nonsense, but "I didn't do it
because I thought it would be immoral" is not.

No wonder we can so easily become puzzled and perplexed
about moral questions.